New Directions for
Higher Education

Martin Kramer and
Judith Block McLaughlin
CO-EDITORS-IN-CHIEF

Institutional Research: More than Just Data

Dawn Geronimo Terkla

EDITOR

Number 141 • Spring 2008
Jossey-Bass
San Francisco

INSTITUTIONAL RESEARCH: MORE THAN JUST DATA
Dawn Geronimo Terkla (ed.)
New Directions for Higher Education, no. 141
Martin Kramer, Judith Block McLaughlin, Co-Editors-in-Chief

Microfilm copies of issues and articles are available in 16mm and 35mm, as well as microfiche in 105mm, through University Microfilms Inc., 300 North Zeeb Road, Ann Arbor, Michigan 48106-1346.

NEW DIRECTIONS FOR HIGHER EDUCATION (ISSN 0271-0560, electronic ISSN 1536-0741) is part of The Jossey-Bass Higher and Adult Education Series and is published quarterly by Wiley Subscription Services, Inc., A Wiley Company, at Jossey-Bass, 989 Market Street, San Francisco, California 94103-1741. Periodicals Postage Paid at San Francisco, California, and at additional mailing offices. POSTMASTER: Send address changes to New Directions for Higher Education, Jossey-Bass, 989 Market Street, San Francisco, California 94103-1741.

New Directions for Higher Education is indexed in Current Index to Journals in Education (ERIC); Higher Education Abstracts.

SUBSCRIPTIONS cost $85 for individuals and $209 for institutions, agencies, and libraries. See ordering information page at end of journal.

EDITORIAL CORRESPONDENCE should be sent to the Co-Editors-in-Chief, Martin Kramer, 2807 Shasta Road, Berkeley, California 94708-2011 and Judith Block McLaughlin, Harvard GSE, Gutman 435, Cambridge, Massachusetts 02138.

Cover photograph © Digital Vision

www.josseybass.com

CONTENTS

prove its worth and help move the university forward. There are specific steps that can be taken at each stage of the process to ensure an optimal outcome.

EDITOR'S NOTES

Institutional research is often one of the best-kept secrets on a college or university campus. Perhaps this is because institutional research offices and institutional researchers tend to be part of the backstage crew that supports the higher education enterprise and its leading cast of characters (e.g., presidents, provosts, deans, and department chairs). Alternatively, perhaps it is because no two institutional research offices are exactly alike. Or maybe institutional research doesn't get the credit it deserves because it is a relatively young profession (the first official offices of institutional research appeared on the higher education horizon in the early 1920s and many colleges and universities didn't add IR offices until the latter part of the twentieth century). Regardless of the precise reason, it is not uncommon for an institutional researcher to be confronted with the query, "What does IR do anyway?"

This volume will demonstrate that institutional researchers do a lot more than collect statistics. They are more than mere "bean counters" (in my particular case a "potato counter"; very early in my career, I was accused by a department chair of counting her faculty like potatoes). Offices of institutional research do deal with data, lots of data, and they generally employ individuals who have a propensity to understand numbers. However, most offices provide services that go beyond merely counting or reporting. Institutional researchers have contributed to creating a culture in higher education of decision-making based on evidence. Institutional researchers are often called upon to provide the information to senior administrators that enables them to make decisions based on factual evidence as opposed to relying entirely on anecdotes.

The eight chapters that comprise this volume are addressed to faculty and administrators who turn to IR offices for support (and those who may not yet do so, but will learn from this volume about the reasons they should). The chapters also provide information and insights that institutional researchers will find valuable as they think about their work.

In Chapter One, J. Fredricks Volkwein states that not all IR offices are created equal. He describes the differing sizes, functions, and structures of institutional research activities and offices and provides a typology of the institutional research landscape that visually depicts the variety of IR offices and structures. Volkwein discusses the characteristics of a mature profession and ponders as to whether institutional research has achieved that status.

In Chapter Two, James F. Trainer discusses the role of institutional research in conducting comparative analyses and benchmarking, to provide

NEW DIRECTIONS FOR HIGHER EDUCATION, no. 141, Spring 2008 © Wiley Periodicals, Inc.
Published online in Wiley InterScience (www.interscience.wiley.com) • DOI: 10.1002/he.288

1

a framework that helps an institution understand where it stands in the higher education landscape. The value of developing a set of peer institutions and the parameters and methodological frameworks that may be employed are discussed. Trainer presents and critiques many sources of comparative data.

Trudy H. Bers, in Chapter Three, identifies ways in which institutional research offices offer leadership and assistance in departmental and institutional efforts to assess student-learning outcomes. She maintains that the credibility of the IR office is a critical asset in helping the institution report its assessment results to external audiences. Impediments that constrain IR effectiveness are also noted.

Chapter Four, by Michael F. Middaugh, Heather A. Kelly, and Allison M. Walters, supports the argument that a comprehensive understanding of faculty workload is critical in assessing institutional effectiveness. The authors present a comprehensive discussion of the many benefits and potential shortcomings of traditional research for faculty workload. They argue persuasively that institutions gain greater insight regarding institution-specific faculty workload and productivity issues if they use detailed information on discipline-specific faculty teaching loads, instructional costs, and externally funded scholarship. Specific examples using data from the Delaware Study of Instructional Costs and Productivity are presented.

Chapter Five, by Anne Marie Delaney, demonstrates how institutional researchers can serve as a valuable resource in enhancing decision-makers' understanding of student populations. Classic institutional research studies about students are described and suggestions are made as to potential use. Further, the chapter reveals how these studies may be employed to evaluate student progress and performance, assess program effectiveness, and increase an institution's competitive advantage.

In Chapter Six, Barbara Brittingham, Patricia M. O'Brien, and Julie L. Alig posit that the accreditation self-study affords an opportunity for IR offices to expand their basic functions, and for academic administrators to expand their usage of data to enhance institutional effectiveness. They offer a number of suggestions regarding how this may be accomplished, including: (1) involving institutional researchers on self-study teams, (2) developing capacity to use data, and (3) evaluating how well the evidence presented worked.

Richard A. Voorhees, in Chapter Seven, argues that a strategic plan that does not make use of data verges on propaganda. According to Voorhees, a plan that uses data to pose goals and formulate strategies more often than not results in a useful framework for gauging an institution's future. He suggests techniques often executed by institutional researchers that colleges and universities should consider as the foundation of their strategic plan.

In Chapter Eight, Jennifer A. Brown discusses the primary activity typically associated with institutional research offices: external reporting.

NEW DIRECTIONS FOR HIGHER EDUCATION • DOI: 10.1002/he

She describes the mandatory federal and state reporting requirements, and identifies many of the major voluntary surveys that institutions comply with each year. Moreover, she raises important questions regarding the impact that the current frenzy for "public disclosure" has on institutional research offices, and she advocates for institutional researchers to become fully engaged partners in the on-going dialogue.

This volume illuminates the many roles and services provided by IR offices. By answering the question, "What do IR offices do," I hope this book will help faculty and administrators realize how institutional research can help them to better understand their institutional environment and make more informed decisions as a result.

Dawn Geronimo Terkla
Editor

DAWN GERONIMO TERKLA is the associate provost for institutional research, assessment, and evaluation at Tufts University and a past president of the Association for Institutional Research and the North East Association for Institutional Research.

1

Do all institutional research offices look alike? This chapter examines the size, function, and structure of institutional research activities and offices across the United States.

The Foundations and Evolution of Institutional Research

J. Fredericks Volkwein

"What is institutional research?"

Almost every IR professional who has been in the field for more than a couple of years can tell a story of being in a crowded elevator between floors at a conference hotel, where someone in the elevator asks that magic question after looking at our name badge. Many of us have given a stammering, perhaps even humorous response to the question. But we do have definitions we can rely on. One of the most widely accepted is by Joe Saupe, who emphasizes institutional research as a set of activities that support institutional planning, policy formation, and decision making (1990).

Years ago, Cameron Fincher at the University of Georgia referred to IR as *organizational intelligence*. Pat Terenzini, my colleague at Penn State, has elaborated on this idea by describing three tiers of organizational intelligence (1999). The first, most basic tier is the *technical and analytical*. This type of intelligence is needed to produce the facts and figures about an institution: admissions, enrollment, degrees awarded, faculty workload, faculty-student ratio—all the elements that add up to describing the basic profile of the institution. Technical and analytical intelligence also includes all the tools of the trade such as spreadsheets, knowledge of statistics, SPSS, and background in survey research. These basic skills are necessary to succeed at an entry level in the profession of institutional research.

Terenzini's second level, on which the first tier is built, is *issues intelligence*. It includes knowledge not just about the technical aspects of the job but also the particular issues facing the institution. Issues such as affirmative action, resource allocation, need for program evaluation, enrollment goal

NEW DIRECTIONS FOR HIGHER EDUCATION, no. 141, Spring 2008 © Wiley Periodicals, Inc.
Published online in Wiley InterScience (www.interscience.wiley.com) • DOI: 10.1002/he.289

setting, and planning are of immediate importance to the institution. It also requires knowing about and working with the key actors and people at the institution who are addressing these issues.

Thus, tier one is more basic than tier two, and tiers one and two are more basic than tier three, which is *contextual intelligence*. The context involves knowing the institution not just internally but externally its history, culture, evolution, external environment within which the institution functions, and trends in that environment such as trends in population of high school graduates and economic health of the state, especially if your institution is primarily state-supported. The sum of contextual intelligence understands all the relevant trends in the external environment: financial, social, political, and demographic.

What are the characteristics of a mature profession, and does IR enjoy these characteristics? We know from such fields as medicine, law, theology, and engineering—the earliest and the most mature of the academic professions—that each field has its own job titles, hierarchy, and common nomenclatures for the subspecializations. We also know that there is similar training as well as degrees and degree titles, and a dominant pattern for career paths. Within each of these mature professions, there are relatively common tasks that the people holding these titles perform, and there are relatively well-oiled quality assurance mechanisms—whether internal, like a medical board that reviews hospital cases, or external, in terms of accreditation review by teams of peers that visit and make judgments about quality and adherence to standards. So the question is whether IR enjoys these same characteristics.

What about professional identity? We know that a huge proportion of the offices in colleges and universities use titles such as institutional research, institutional studies, and institutional analysis. We see an array of other titles as well. Institutional researchers and IR functions are imbedded in the offices of strategic planning, institutional management, assessment, evaluation, budget analysis, enrollment management, enrollment research, and planning. "Institutional effectiveness" is a common title I have seen lately. But it is important to recognize that IR, whatever it is called, is not necessarily limited to colleges and universities. We know that foundations, government bureaus, state education departments, and research-oriented organizations are increasingly hiring people with training in institutional research (Figure 1.1).

If you look across the U.S. higher education landscape, you will see that at most institutions there are strong connections, if not formal organizational arrangements, uniting the people in (1) institutional research and analysis; (2) planning and budgeting; and (3) assessment, effectiveness, and accreditation. I think of these three as the golden triangle of institutional research because they dominate most of the practice of IR in the United States (Figure 1.2).

NEW DIRECTIONS FOR HIGHER EDUCATION • DOI: 10.1002/he

Figure 1.1. Common Words Appearing in IR Office Titles

- Research
- Institutional research
- Research and information
- Research and planning
- Strategic planning
- Academic planning
- Institutional planning

- Assessment
- Evaluation
- Analysis
- Budget analysis
- Effectiveness
- Institutional effectiveness
- Enrollment management
- Enrollment research and planning

Figure 1.2. Golden Triangle

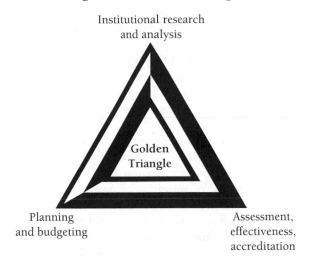

Institutional research
and analysis

Golden
Triangle

Planning
and budgeting

Assessment,
effectiveness,
accreditation

The Evolution of IR

In the last chapter of *New Directions for Institutional Research* volume 104, Marvin Peterson (1999) discusses the evolution of institutional research as a profession. He places it within the context of the larger changes occurring within society and higher education. Certainly, the changes in higher education over the decades have been remarkable. Our economy has grown in the last hundred years or so from being dominated by agriculture and then by industry, to now being much more knowledge-based. Our social values transitioned from being very elitist, where we offered education for the few, to being very meritocratic, where we thought of education as something for the most deserving and the most talented. But now we are more egalitarian, emphasizing education for all. Our organizational structures have gone from being administration-centered, bureaucratic, and formal a century ago to becoming, several decades ago, much more open and faculty-centered. Now,

NEW DIRECTIONS FOR HIGHER EDUCATION • DOI: 10.1002/he

I think it is fair to say many institutions of higher education are much more client-centered and learner-centered. This is congruent also with changing credentials; we've gone from a period of time when a high school diploma was the most valued workplace credential, and then the bachelor's degree was the necessary minimum. Now we can see that in many fields of endeavor one needs a master's or doctoral degree to have a fulfilling or enduring career.

Our governance structures in higher education a century ago were dominated by private institutions; then during the middle of the past century we transitioned toward public higher education, led by establishment of thousands of community colleges and state universities. Now our governing structures are increasingly statewide and systemwide, embracing cooperative, consortia, and interinstitutional arrangements that emphasize collaboration as well as distance education providers that increasingly compete with bricks-and-mortar campuses.

Also congruent with this trend has been the shift in areas such as budgeting, accountability, and performance. In budgeting, we've gone from a period when budgets were largely endowment-based to seeing them largely formula-based, particularly in state systems; now, budgets are much more likely to be performance-based. Thus the changed accountability atmosphere has gone from one emphasizing resources and reputation—the old accountability model—to a period when for a while we were concentrating on goal attainment and program evaluation and processes, such as student ratings of instruction, and now much more emphasis on results, outputs, and outcomes. During this period, our IR offices and staff have been pulled more directly into helping reshape, redirect, and refine their institutions. They analyze the surrounding environment responsively to pressure for demonstrating performance and results. For example, conducting economic impact studies is now highly a common activity in the office. This activity blends internal and external elements.

So the primary role of IR has changed over time from emphasizing and requiring primarily descriptive statistics, fact books, and reporting to more analysis and evaluation, both quantitative and qualitative. Today there is a demand for IR skills requiring multivariate analysis and modeling: forecasts of revenues, enrollment projections, analysis of policy issues, and modeling alternative scenarios of tuition and financial aid and their impact on admissions attractiveness and therefore on enrollments. These are examples of steady changes that have accelerated dramatically in the past ten years (Figure 1.3).

Some of these trends have been confirmed by various surveys of Association for Institutional Research (AIR) members. We have a survey of the membership under way in 2008, but the two studies in 1992 and 1998 seen in Figure 1.3 are consistent with Peterson's observations (1999). There has been a growth in the emphasis on accountability and performance, reporting

Figure 1.3. Topics of High Importance to AIR Members

Topic	1992	1998	
Outcomes assessment	53%	61%	
Research design and analysis	50%	52%	
Persistence and retention	48%	63%	
Management issues	42%	32%	
Enrollment management	35%	39%	
Financial issues	25%	21%	
Minority and diversity issues	25%	19%	
Faculty issues	24%	22%	
Student affairs issues	13%	15%	
Accountability and performance indicators		71%	
Technology issues		63%	
Information systems and data management		63%	
Efficiency issues		36%	

Source: Sarah Lindquist, "A Profile of Institutional Researchers from AIR National Membership Surveys" from J. F. Volkwein (ed.), *New Directions for Institutional Research*, #104, Winter 1999.

on technology and knowledge management, information systems, outcomes assessment, and studies of persistence and retention. Institutional researchers report that these items are becoming increasingly important in their jobs.

We must be cautious in generalizing about the practice of institutional research, because we know that organizational arrangements are highly variable from campus to campus and state to state. The most common pattern is for IR to report to the chief academic officer, someone with the title of provost or vice president for academic affairs. In this situation, the office is usually shaped heavily toward conducting studies of faculty workload, faculty salary equity, student ratings of instruction, and other elements directly connected to the instructional and academic side of the institution. Many other IR offices report to the president or chancellor. This is especially true when "planning" appears in the title of the office or in the person's job description, and in relatively small institutions (Figure 1.4).

In some cases, the chief financial officer hires institutional researchers to engage in budget analysis and resource allocation studies. Development and alumni operations are increasingly hiring institutional research officers to help them with activities and analysis that support fundraising and alumni development. Perhaps the biggest growth area is in student affairs. The 1998 total of 4 percent of IR offices within student affairs, I believe, underrepresents the patterns out there in the environment that I've observed in the last ten years. Chief student affairs officers on many campuses are

Figure 1.4. IR Location in Organizational Structure

Academic Affairs/Provost	38%
President/Chancellor	26%
Business Affairs/Services	8%
Development/Alumni	5%
Student Affairs/Services	4%
Other	18%

Source: Sarah Lindquist, "A Profile of Institutional Researchers from AIR National Membership Surveys" from J. F. Volkwein (ed.), *New Directions for Institutional Research*, #104, Winter 1999.

hiring professionals to help them engage in studies of campus climate, residential life, freshmen year experience, retention and diversity, and effectiveness of student services and how they might be improved. This is another growth area within the larger picture of IR. One generalization that is safe to make is that the practice of institutional research tends to be shaped by the part of the organization that it is located in. As a result, if IR is in student services it is more likely to be doing studies of student life and campus climate. If IR is lodged in academic affairs it is much more likely to be engaged in studies of faculty workload, salary equity, and faculty research and scholarship. If it is in finance and business it is much more likely to be carrying out studies that support the resource allocation process and making revenue projections (Figure 1.5).

Figure 1.5. AIR Member's Preparation and Experience

	1989	2003	
Highest degree			
Doctorate	33%	38%	
Master's	46%	53%	
Field of highest degree			
Social sciences	39%	38%	
Education	26%	37%	
Math and science	14%	8%	
Business	11%	13%	
Humanities	8%	5%	
Years of experience in IR			
0–2	27	16%	
3–5	27	23%	
6–10	21	25%	
11+	25	35%	

Source: J. F. Volkwein (ed.), *New Directions for Institutional Research*.

There is some modest evidence for the growing maturity of the profession in terms of degree attainment and experience level of members of AIR, as reported in two surveys, one in the late 1980s and the other in 2003. The proportions of those with a doctorate or master's degree have risen. The number of IR professionals with only a few years of experience has declined, whereas the number with more than a decade of experience has increased over this time period. Consequently, IR is becoming a career for more IR practitioners, and the level of educational training seems to be steadily increasing. The field still draws heavily upon those with a background in the social sciences. We know that many IR practitioners come from psychology and sociology, and increasing numbers are coming into institutional research with a background in a field such as economics or even anthropology. But the traditional route is to come to institutional research through the field of education. This may be because of the increasing number of higher education programs offering a specialization in IR, as at Penn State. The number of people coming from math and sciences and from humanities has dropped modestly over the years. There has been a small increase of those coming into IR with a background in business, usually with an MBA degree (Figure 1.6).

Suggesting the diversity of IR as a profession, John Muffo (1999) summarized the IR studies of regional and state organizations. In separate studies in separate years, Canada, Northeast AIR, New England, SAIR, and Georgia show dramatically differing IR office sizes, with an average of five

Figure 1.6. Characteristics of Institutional Research Offices

Region	Year	Mean IR Size	Administrative Reporting Area	Headed by Doctoral Degree	Dominant Tasks
Canada n = 27	1990	5.5	President (15%) Academic VP (11%) Other (74%)	15%	Enrollment analysis, Compile statistics
Northeast n = 141	1990	1.3	President (40%) Academic VP (25%) Other (35%)	52%	Enrollment management, External reporting
New England n = 127	1997	1.0	President (34%) Academic VP (38%) Other (28%)	18%	Enrollment analysis, Institutional reporting
South n = 240	1995	4.5	President (24%) Academic VP (34%) Other (42%)	56%	Institutional planning, External reporting
Georgia n = 54	1994	3.0	President (55%) Academic VP (27%) Other (18%)	37%	National surveys, Affirmative action

Source: John Muffo, "A Comparison of Findings from Regional Studies of Institutional Research Offices" from J. F. Volkwein (ed.), *New Directions for Institutional Research*, #104, Winter 1999.

NEW DIRECTIONS FOR HIGHER EDUCATION • DOI: 10.1002/he

people per office in Canada and four in the South, whereas an office of only one or two persons is quite common in New England and the Northeast. This may say something about institutional size as well as the diversity of reporting arrangements. Smaller offices are more likely to report to the president, while the larger offices are more likely to report to some official other than the president. In the South and Northeast, offices are most likely to be headed by someone with a doctoral degree. It looks as if enrollment management and external reporting are almost universals for practicing members of AIR.

We also know from other studies of the AIR membership that the practice of institutional research is highly variable. Institutional researchers find themselves in offices in various parts of their organization, some more academically oriented and others more financially oriented, some oriented toward students and student studies and some more toward planning and enrollment management. We also know that these offices differ in structure and culture. The practice of IR varies greatly across the country.

An Institutional Research Ecology. Beginning in 1990 and continuing through 2008, I have been collecting information from IR colleagues about the structure and functions of their offices, and I am finding that the arrangements are highly variable. Some of the offices are fairly new and underdeveloped, sometimes with a single person who has been pulled out of the faculty and given the IR assignment by the president or provost. I see large offices that are relatively well established and have gained the confidence of the president and the provost over time.

I have studied other campuses where institutional research is highly fragmented and activities take place in many pockets and corners of the campus. I developed a typology to explain this ecology. I see *craft structures* as fitting a surprisingly large number of one- and two-person offices that are highly burdened by mandated routine reporting and a modest amount of number crunching for the institution. Many IR people in craft structures do not have a doctoral degree, but others do hold advanced degrees, especially if they are former faculty members. These people and offices dominate the ranks of institutions that have an enrollment under five thousand (Figure 1.7).

Most craft structures evolve and grow into what I call *small adhocracies*. These are the two- and three-person offices grown out of childhood and into a more adolescent and maybe even entrepreneurial stage. A flat hierarchy, simple structure, and minimal specialization characterize offices at this stage of development. The tasks of small adhocracies and the credentials of the staff also vary highly from one campus to another. Some are engaged in applied research projects, and some not. Some of their staff members have a doctoral degree, but most have a master's degree and work experience. Small adhocracies are highly responsive to their administrative hosts and account for at least 30 percent of the IR offices in the Northeast. They carry

Figure 1.7. Ecology of Institutional Research Offices

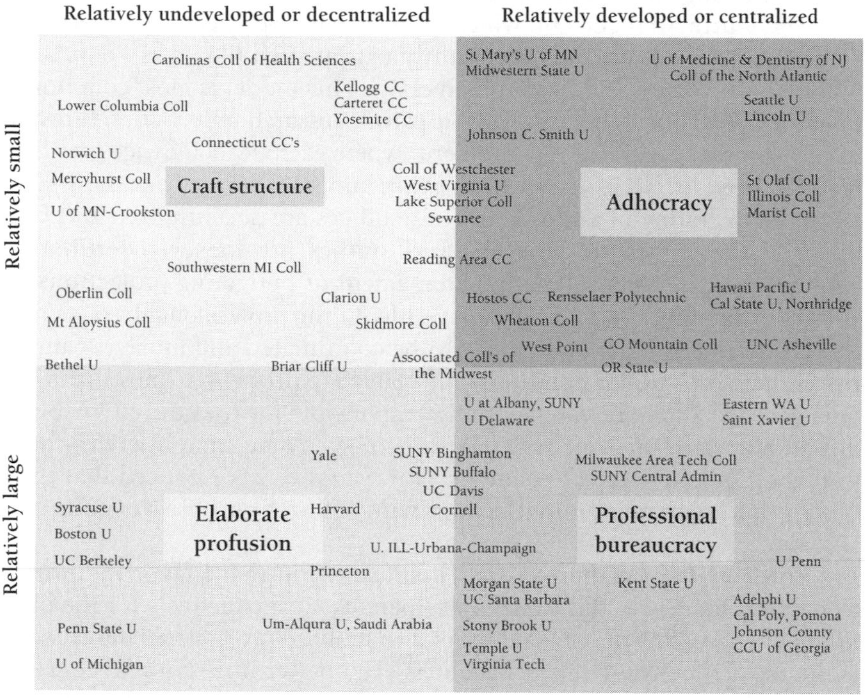

Relatively undeveloped or decentralized   Relatively developed or centralized

Relatively small

Carolinas Coll of Health Sciences

Lower Columbia Coll

Norwich U
Mercyhurst Coll
U of MN-Crookston

Craft structure

Connecticut CC's

Kellogg CC
Carteret CC
Yosemite CC

St Mary's U of MN
Midwestern State U

U of Medicine & Dentistry of NJ
Coll of the North Atlantic

Seattle U
Lincoln U

Johnson C. Smith U

Coll of Westchester
West Virginia U
Lake Superior Coll
Sewanee

Adhocracy

St Olaf Coll
Illinois Coll
Marist Coll

Southwestern MI Coll

Oberlin Coll
Mt Aloysius Coll

Bethel U

Reading Area CC

Clarion U

Skidmore Coll

Briar Cliff U

Hostos CC   Rensselaer Polytechnic
Wheaton Coll

West Point   CO Mountain Coll
Associated Coll's of   OR State U
the Midwest

Hawaii Pacific U
Cal State U, Northridge

UNC Asheville

U at Albany, SUNY
U Delaware

Eastern WA U
Saint Xavier U

Relatively large

Syracuse U
Boston U
UC Berkeley

Elaborate profusion

Yale

Harvard

Princeton

SUNY Binghamton
SUNY Buffalo
UC Davis
Cornell

U. ILL-Urbana-Champaign

Milwaukee Area Tech Coll
SUNY Central Admin

Professional bureaucracy

U Penn

Penn State U

U of Michigan

Um-Alqura U, Saudi Arabia

Morgan State U
UC Santa Barbara
Stony Brook U
Temple U
Virginia Tech

Kent State U

Adelphi U
Cal Poly, Pomona
Johnson County
CCU of Georgia

out activities that are highly focused on the part of the organization they are in—for example, academic affairs, business and finance, student affairs, or some other part of the organization.

Small adhocracies often grow into what I call *professional bureaucracies*. They most commonly occur when IR offices and IR activities are centralized on a campus in a single office. Professional bureaucracy represents a more formal IR arrangement of at least four professionals and usually more. I've seen offices of six, ten, and even twenty people. Professionals with a doctorate and many years of experience dominate the professional bureaucracy. These offices have developed a modest bureaucratic structure in terms of hierarchy, division of labor, and specialization. The professional bureaucracy version of IR usually has more than one person with a doctorate, plus more than one person with ten or more years of experience. These offices often have several entry-level positions, occupied by graduate assistants and others with a master's degree who may be just getting started in the field of IR. These offices carry out the most sophisticated research projects, which are likely to be centralized in the IR office rather than conducted by another office with IR participation. I know from national meetings that these offices constitute the model most of us mentally picture when we think about IR.

NEW DIRECTIONS FOR HIGHER EDUCATION • DOI: 10.1002/he

However, the professional bureaucracy probably accounts for only one-quarter of the IR arrangements nationally.

The fourth arrangement, which I call *elaborate profusion,* is where IR is spread across campus. This is certainly true at such places as Penn State, Syracuse University, and Boston University. This model is most common at research universities, and especially at private research universities. It results from a complex analytical environment, where each dean and vice president feels the need for his or her own expertise and staff to carry out these studies, often operating in a silo. Thus these offices are decentralized and fragmented. Sometimes IR activities and studies are loosely coordinated, whether they are in enrollment management or budgeting projections, or studies of campus climate and student life. In the professional bureaucracy, these studies are much more likely to be coordinated and involve teams of researchers, but under conditions of elaborate profusion the studies frequently have a lone researcher being responsible for the study. Obviously, not all offices fit into one part of this ecology. Some campuses may be in transition from one type to another. However, I've have noticed that these descriptions seem to capture the dominant patterns we observe in the field IR today.

You may have gathered from this discussion that I favor the professional bureaucracy as the model that operates most effectively for the practice of effective IR. Not only do I think a centralized professional bureaucracy is the most effective; I also believe it is even better if this office reports to the president or the chief executive officer of the institution. I have visited campuses that place IR functions into separate offices, but the centralized IR model is more efficient and more effective, I believe, because it takes advantage of natural economies of scale that are associated with shared expertise, cross-training, and methodological diversity. Also, a centralized arrangement protects the institution better against the inefficiency of narrow specialization and the service gaps resulting from staff turnover, health problems, and family emergency. Any particular function or task that you can identify—student tracking, survey research, space utilization, instructional workload analysis, enrollment forecasting—can be better supported in a centralized operation because of the backup that comes with cross-training. What is the likelihood in a given office that on any particular day or week someone is going to be absent because of illness or vacation or family emergency? In such absence, whatever that person is working on comes to a halt, *except* in a large office where you have cross-training and teamwork and many people involved in the project instead of just one. Effective teamwork takes place only in a relatively large centralized operation, and it is usually missing from a fragmented one where IR is scattered across the institution in a series of smaller offices (Figure 1.8).

This model IR organizational chart shows the core functions of institutional research divided into areas that are each the responsibility of a

Figure 1.8. IR Organized by Function (Most Common Arrangement)

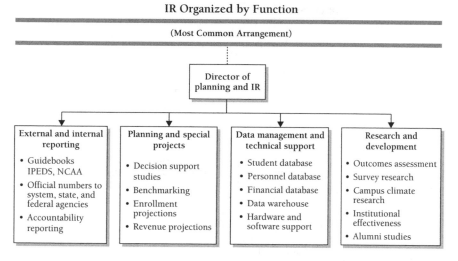

well-trained, if not experienced, analyst. Someone needs to be the lead person in compiling the official facts and figures about the institution, both internally and externally. Someone needs to be the "go to" person for key decision-support studies, especially those supporting campus planning. Someone needs to be the center of gravity for ongoing data management and technical support, and to act as the office liaison with IT and the many offices that have supplied data to the campus data warehouse. And someone needs to supply the research design and multivariate statistical skills for the office, and act as the local expert on survey research, evaluation, and assessment. Naturally, the director of the office should also have some of these skills. Most offices and most effective operations require full-time analysts in each area, allowing the director to lead and coordinate and be an important contributor to the campus management team as well as being a researcher. This works only when there are other people around in a centralized operation to pick up the slack for turnover or absence for one reason or another.

An alternative version of the IR professional bureaucracy again is centralized, but instead of being organized by function it is organized by its major customers—its major information customers (Figure 1.9). The benefit of this arrangement is that each major part of the organization knows there is a person they can go to if they want information. If the provost's office needs a study of faculty workload, salary equity analysis, or indicators of faculty activity and effort, there is an IR contact person to serve that need, regardless of whatever background the person may have in other areas (survey research, multivariate statistics, other training). Similarly, the chief financial officer knows there is a person in the office he or she can go to in

Figure 1.9. IR Organized by Customer (Highly Effective)

IR Organized by Customer (Highly Effective)

IR director

Tech support and data warehousing

Academic Affairs support	Business/Finance support	Enrollment management	Student Affairs support
• Compile indicators of quality/effectiveness • Faculty workload • Student ratings of instruction • Faculty salary analysis • Faculty publications, citations, honors, awards, service	• Compile indicators of productivity/ efficiency/cost • Revenue projections • Tuition pricing studies • Fundraising analysis • Resource allocation criteria	• Admissions marketing Studies • Financial aid analysis • Enrollment projections • Retention/graduation estimates • Alumni studies	• Quality of residential life • Student satisfaction surveys • Diversity and campus climate • Athletics research

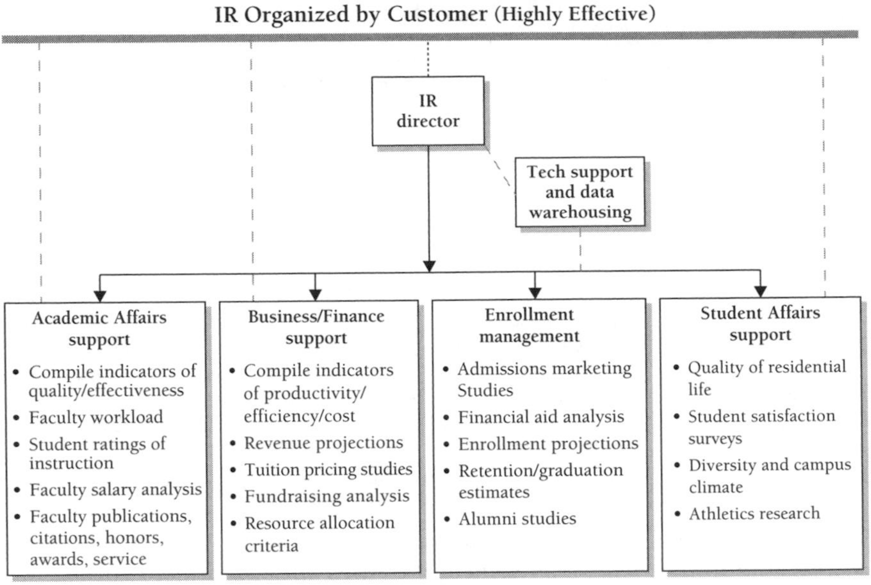

doing a tuition pricing analysis or looking at the balance between tuition and financial aid and what that might do to revenue. There is an enrollment management person who works with offices of financial aid and admissions primarily and does follow-up studies in retention and graduation, and perhaps even alumni research. Finally, there is the student affairs support person, who works with student affairs on everything from satisfaction surveys to studies of campus climate and diversity, athletics, and quality of residential life. When needed, each can take the lead for a project, or work as a team because they have cross training and expertise that cut across these areas. Usually, in this arrangement there is a single person responsible for data warehousing and technical support. This is an alternative arrangement that emphasizes customer service and makes sure all the key decision makers on the campus are getting the information they need.

The Maturation Process. So what is the verdict? Is IR a mature profession? We see that it has many organizational arrangements. People come into the field with highly variable training, background, and earned degrees. There is a core of common tasks, but they too depend on what part of the organization IR is lodged in. Also, career patterns and career paths appear to vary considerably. IR has begun to develop its own training and quality assurance mechanisms through summer institutes and the IR certificate program, as is the case with my own program at Penn State. The general consensus about the skills IR practitioners need is that this shapes hiring practices, but only indirectly. There is no IR curriculum or "accreditation" today.

NEW DIRECTIONS FOR HIGHER EDUCATION • DOI: 10.1002/he

On the other hand, we have several mature AIR publications that form the knowledge base for the field. The best of them, I believe, is *New Directions for Institutional Research* (NDIR), a topic-based source book published by Jossey-Bass, with an AIR editor since 1974. NDIR reflects the richness and diversity of IR subjects and methodologies, and it recently grew from four volumes per year to five. The official scholarly journal for AIR, published since 1972, is *Research in Higher Education,* which is now perhaps the most selective journal in the field. Started in 1985, the *Higher Education Handbook* publishes one annual volume and is jointly sponsored by AIR and the Association for the Study of Higher Education. The *Handbook* is organized around twelve to fifteen higher education topic areas, each with its own associate editor. Additional publications resources are the *Primer* for IR, which is updated periodically (Knight, 2003); the *AIR Professional File, AIR Currents,* and *Resources in Institutional Research,* a series of AIR monographs published annually; and *Assessment in the Disciplines,* also an annual series aimed at both faculty and institutional researchers who support student learning assessment.

Moreover, AIR has and has had for many years an effective and thorough statement of ethics for the profession. So maybe it is safe to say that maturity is relative and the field is gradually evolving toward a state of greater maturity from its infancy of thirty to forty years ago, when it began as a field of practice but now continues as more a field of study.

The Faces of Institutional Research

Thus we conclude that IR is an evolving profession, and one of its realities is the difference between the IR administrative role (in which you act as a member of the administration and a member of the management team) and the professional role (which is more academic and scholarly and emphasizes the need for impartial and objective research). These contradictory dualities and tensions force us to play a medley of roles. My own experience led me to identify four "faces" of institutional research (1999), shown in modified form in Figure 1.10.

In the heading above the boxes, I distinguish among those IR purposes, roles, and activities that are internal, formative, and improvement-oriented rather than external, summative, and accountability-oriented. On the left side of the boxes, I characterize the organizational culture and value system in two ways: academic and professional versus administrative and institutional. This produces a typology of four overlapping yet distinguishable types of IR purposes and roles. These are not pure types but reflect dominant tendencies, and they can be applied either to the office as a whole or to the separate individuals and functions within.

In their *New Directions for IR* volume 113, Andreea Serban and Jing Luan have improved my four faces by adding a fifth: IR as knowledge manager.

Figure 1.10. Five Faces of Institutional Research

Organizational Role and Culture	Purposes and Audiences	
	Formative and Internal, for Improvement	Summative and External, for Accountability
Administrative and institutional	To describe the institution; IR as information authority	To present the best case; IR as spin doctor
Academic and professional	To analyze alternatives; IR as policy analyst	To supply impartial evidence of effectiveness; IR as scholar and researcher
Technology	To gather and transform data into information and knowledge; to collaborate in creating and maintaining information repositories and to facilitate the process of knowledge creation, capture, and sharing; IR as knowledge manager	

Source: Andrea Serban (2002), "Knowledge Management: The Fifth Face of Institutional Research," J. F. Volkwein (ed.), *New Directions for Institutional Research*, #113, Jossey-Bass, San Francisco.

I like their enhancement and believe that creation and management of knowledge is a form of organizational intelligence that fertilizes all the others.

IR as Information Authority. The internal and more administrative purpose and support role calls on institutional research to describe the shape and size of the institution, its students and staff, and its activities. Here the institutional researcher educates the campus community in terms of data on admissions, enrollment, faculty, and degrees awarded. Generating most of the information in the factbook falls into this category. In this role, the institutional researcher compiles and packages descriptive statistics for campus audiences. Of the many challenging IR tasks, this one probably requires the least preparation in the form of education and experience. The role requirements correspond roughly to Terenzini's technical intelligence (1999).

IR as Policy Analyst. The internal and more professional purpose calls on IR to study and analyze the institution and its policies. In this role, the institutional researcher works with top management as an analyst or consultant by supporting planning and budget allocation decisions, policy revision, administrative restructuring, and other needed changes. Here the institutional researcher is the policy analyst who educates the management team. Many of us are especially likely to assume this role as we conduct studies for our colleagues in academic affairs, budgeting, and student services. Studies that give alternative enrollment scenarios and revenue projections based on particular assumptions about inputs and attrition fall into this category. Comparative cost analysis, student opinion research, and studies of salary equity are other examples. This role requires a relatively high level of education and training, as well as analytical and issues intelligence.

IR as Spin Doctor. Of the two external types, the more administrative style is visible when IR assembles descriptive statistics that reflect favorably on the institution. Many of us are called on to play this advocate role frequently, and we need to protect against carrying this style to an unethical extreme. Here, the IR staff presents the best case for the campus, describing the glass as half full rather than half empty. Some would put our admissions material for students and parents in this category, but we certainly perform this role in assisting campus fundraising and government relations staff in presenting a positive image. Some experience on the job and knowledge of the institution is usually needed for success in this role.

IR as Scholar/Researcher. The more professionally oriented and analytic version of the external or accountability role is that of the impartial researcher and scholar who investigates and produces evidence so that institutional effectiveness, legal compliance, and goal attainment can be judged. Conducting outcomes studies and performance reports when the primary audience is external to the campus falls into this category. Support for the accreditation self-study might be another example. This is a sophisticated role that requires advanced training and years of experience.

Some IR activities are difficult to classify because they overlap several categories. The factbook has both internal and external audiences. Compliance reporting has descriptive and analytical aspects. When we score and

Figure 1.11. Volkwein's IR: The Guiding Light

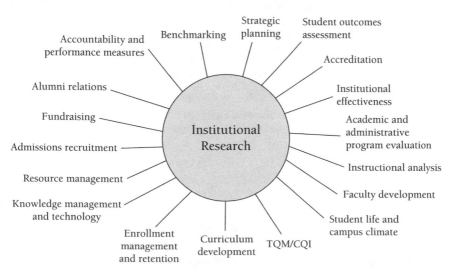

report student ratings, we act as the information authority, but we become the research analyst as we carry out studies based on student ratings data. Faculty workload and instructional analysis can appear in all four boxes of Figure 1.10, depending on the audience and the complexity of the task.

Nevertheless, most of what we do forces us to play one or another of these roles, sometimes simultaneously. Although the boundaries around these four faces of institutional research may blur from time to time, and the transition from one to the other can be as rapid as a telephone call, I'm convinced that my institution needs IR to play all four roles effectively. I suspect that your institution does too.

Thus we see that institutional research is the guiding light or center of gravity for all of the university's analytical activities—internal and external, formative and summative, administrative and academic. By showing all these faces, IR can indeed be the guiding light or rising sun that shines its rays into every corner of the institution (Figure 1.11).

References

Knight, W. E. (ed.). *Primer for Institutional Research.* Resources in Institutional Research no. 14. Tallahassee, Fla.: Association for Institutional Research, 2003.

Muffo, J. A. "A Comparison of Findings from Regional Studies of Institutional Research Offices." In J. F. Volkwein (ed.), *What Is Institutional Research All About? A Critical and Comprehensive Assessment of the Profession.* New Directions in Institutional Research, no. 104. San Francisco: Jossey-Bass, 1999.

Peterson, M. W. "The Role of Institutional Research: From Improvement to Redesign." In J. F. Volkwein (ed.), *What Is Institutional Research All About? A Critical and Comprehensive Assessment of the Profession.* New Directions in Institutional Research, no. 104. San Francisco: Jossey-Bass, 1999.

Saupe, J. L. *The Functions of Institutional Research* (2nd ed.), 1990. Available at http://www.airweb.org/page.asp?page=85.

Terenzini, P. T. "On the Nature of Institutional Research and the Knowledge and Skills It Requires." In J. F. Volkwein (ed.), *What Is Institutional Research All About? A Critical and Comprehensive Assessment of the Profession.* New Directions in Institutional Research, no. 104. San Francisco: Jossey-Bass, 1999.

Volkwein, J. F. "The Four Faces of Institutional Research." In J. F. Volkwein (ed.), *What Is Institutional Research All About? A Critical and Comprehensive Assessment of the Profession.* New Directions in Institutional Research, no. 104. San Francisco: Jossey-Bass, 1999.

Volkwein, J. F. (ed.). *What Is Institutional Research All About? A Critical and Comprehensive Assessment of the Profession.* New Directions for Institutional Research, no. 104. San Francisco: Jossey-Bass, 1999.

J. FREDERICKS VOLKWEIN is a professor in the Center for the Study of Higher Education at Penn State and for the past fifteen years has served as either the editor or associate editor of New Directions for Institutional Research.

2

In the age of Google, data appear to be plentiful. The secret is knowing where to obtain useful and relevant data, how to access them, and how to draw meaningful conclusions from them.

The Role of Institutional Research in Conducting Comparative Analysis of Peers

James F. Trainer

In this age of accountability, transparency, and accreditation, colleges and universities increasingly conduct comparative analyses and engage in benchmarking activities. Meant to inform institutional planning and decision making, comparative analyses and benchmarking are employed to let stakeholders know how an institution stacks up against its peers and, more likely, a set of aspirant institutions—those that organizational leaders seek to emulate. Boards of trustees, faculty, alumni, accrediting bodies, bonding agencies, and coordinating bodies are among those interested in comparative data. Entire cottage industries have developed to feed the need for benchmarking data and analyses. Volumes have been written on defining and selecting comparison groups, on accessing comparative data and conducting comparative analyses. Comparative analyses, according to McLaughlin and Howard (2005), permit evaluating competition, providing benchmarks, identifying areas of weakness, guiding policy development, and justifying such things as budget requests, salary adjustments, teaching loads, and tuition increases.

This chapter introduces the topic of comparative analyses and benchmarking. It looks at how to select a comparison group and where to find (and how to access) comparative data. It discusses data sharing consortia and

The author is indebted to Stephen A. Sheridan, assistant director for institutional research in the Office of Planning, Training, and Institutional Research at Villanova University, for his assistance in preparing and reviewing this chapter.

formal data sharing arrangements of various sorts. It draws on the work of Paul Brinkman (1987), Deborah Teeter (1983), Teeter and Brinkman (2003), as well as the volume *Inter-institutional Data Exchange: When to Do It, What to Look for and How to Make It Work* (Fergerson, 1996), published by Jossey-Bass as a part of the New Directions for Institutional Research series.

Choosing Comparison Institutions

Teeter and Brinkman (2003) note that comparison groups generally fall into four distinct, albeit not completely mutually exclusive, categories, some of which contain further subcategories. Comparison groups can be thought of as being predetermined, as groups of competitor or aspiration institutions, or as groups of true peer institutions. Each basic comparison group can prove to be helpful, although each type has both strengths and weaknesses.

Predetermined comparison groups include those institutions with which an institution already shares an association for reasons beyond mere comparative purposes. Predetermined comparison groups may include, as Teeter and Brinkman note, institutions that have a natural or traditional affiliation with each other, fall within the same jurisdiction as each other, or are classified together for some reason in some other way. Institutions that have a natural affiliation with each other may be members of the same athletic conference, share a common religious heritage, or be located in the same geographic area or region of the country. Institutions with a traditional affiliation generally share similar histories. Institutions located within the same state or other political boundary (county, city, and so on) are thought of as jurisdictional peers. Institutional peers, on the basis of classification, include those institutions grouped similarly in classification schemes such as those developed and maintained by the Carnegie Foundation for the Advancement of Teaching (Carnegie) and the American Association of University Professors (AAUP).

Competitor groups are those institutions that compete with one another for students, faculty, and staff, and other resources including finances. An aspirant group consists of those institutions that an institution seeks to emulate. They often include colleges and universities that currently outperform an institution in the competition for students, faculty, and other resources. Peer institutions are those institutions that are "similar in role, scope and/or mission" (Teeter and Brinkman, 2003, pp. 106).

Although the benefits of each aforementioned group may be readily apparent, the weaknesses may not be. For instance, even though predetermined groups may be highly visible and widely accepted, one must evaluate whether these groups are appropriate for specific comparisons. Similarly, jurisdictional peers are often grouped together in politically charged situations (budget and resource allocation, state level policy development, and so forth) and may share little else beyond being found within the same political boundary. In the same way, presenting an aspirational group of schools

NEW DIRECTIONS FOR HIGHER EDUCATION • DOI: 10.1002/he

as a set of "peer" institutions may lack credibility with intended audiences. Competitor institutions may not be similar to one another in mission, size, scope, or complexity. Finally, groups formed on the basis of classification criteria typically share only a few characteristics while allowing wide variation on other important institutional dimensions (McLaughlin and Howard, 2005). Suffice it to say it is important to take care in selecting, employing, and presenting institutions that may be used for comparative purposes.

Identifying peer groups, Teeter and Brinkman contend, occurs along a methodological continuum rooted in subjective judgment at one end and high-level statistical analyses at the other. Between these extremes lie approaches that rely on a combination of judgment, data, and statistical analyses to varying degrees. Peer selection methods based purely on statistical analyses generally involve cluster, factor, and discriminant analytic techniques. These selections are viewed as being fully objective. Selection based on judgment, on the other hand, involves convening panels of institutional experts to deliberate on and choose comparison institutions. Threshold and hybrid approaches lie between the judgment and purely analytical means of selecting peers. An excerpt from Teeter and Brinkman (2003) is particularly instructive in understanding the distinctions between the various methodologies and typologies used in selecting peers:

> Cluster analysis and supporting factor-analytic and discriminant techniques are characterized by heavy reliance on multivariate statistics and computer processing. An advantage of cluster analysis is that a large number of institutional descriptors can be readily handled. These statistical techniques tend to de-emphasize the judgment of administrator input. The hybrid approach incorporates a strong emphasis on data and on input from administrators, combined with statistical algorithms for manipulating data. The threshold approach also emphasizes a formal, systematic approach to data and to administrator input; however it depends little, if at all, on statistical algorithms. In the panel approach, administrator input is heavily emphasized; some data may be included informally, but not systematically or comprehensively [p. 107].

Regardless of the approach employed in identifying comparison institutions and in conducting comparative analyses, one must have access to data before any steps in selection or analysis can be fully pursued. In the next section, we examine various sources of comparative data. However, before turning attention to accessing comparative data, it might be helpful to a take a look at a relatively new system developed by Carnegie for identifying and grouping similar institutions.

Many readers are probably familiar with the basic Carnegie classification scheme, dating back to the 1970s and most recently updated in 2006, which classifies institutions according to the number and levels of degrees they award, and for doctorate degree-granting institutions their level of research activity. A newer system developed by Carnegie and released in 2005 illustrates, as the foundation notes,

> a range of ways to think about how colleges and universities resemble or differ from one another. The new classifications offer a set of different lenses through which to view higher education. Each institution appears in each of the new classifications.
>
> The new classifications are organized around three key questions: What is taught? To whom? In what setting? Two of the new classifications focus on the instructional program (one on the undergraduate program, and one on the graduate program). Two describe the profile of enrolled students (one describes the mix of undergraduate and graduate/professional students, while the other focuses on the undergraduate population). Finally, a fifth differentiates institutions with respect to size and residential character.

Taken together, the five dimensions of the new classification scheme help to identify institutions that are similar to each other in a number of ways. A custom listing tool and various filters available on the Carnegie classification Website (http://www.carnegiefoundation.org/classifications/index.asp) affords users the opportunity to even further tailor groupings of institutions.

Sources of Comparative Data

With the advent of the World Wide Web, those interested in conducting comparative analyses for colleges and universities have little difficulty finding data to employ in their activities. Large sums of comparative data are readily available from publicly accessible sources such as state and federal databases. Indeed, data from the Integrated Postsecondary Data System (IPEDS), maintained by the federal Department of Education's National Center for Educational Statistics (NCES), may be sufficient to meet many of our comparative data needs. This system and its components are described in greater detail in sections that follow. Other sources of comparative data include, but are not limited to, organizations that conduct national surveys, membership associations and advocacy groups, special interest Websites, guide book publishers, various proprietary organizations, and formal data sharing consortia.

According to the IPEDS Website (http://www.nces.ed.gov/ipeds/), "IPEDS is the core postsecondary education data collection program for NCES. Data are collected from all primary providers of postsecondary education in the country in areas including enrollments, program completions, graduation rates, faculty, staff, finances, institutional prices, and student financial aid." Data are made available through the IPEDS Website to students, researchers, and others. The data in the IPEDS database are drawn from eight surveys that colleges and universities are required to submit to NCES, covering topics such as enrollment, degree completion, finances, financial aid, graduation rate, human resources, and institutional characteristics.

NEW DIRECTIONS FOR HIGHER EDUCATION • DOI: 10.1002/he

Once in the IPEDS database, data are available for comparative purposes via five data tools, described by IPEDS:

1. The Peer Analysis System (PAS), which enables a user to compare any chosen institution to a group of peer institutions on selected variables
2. The Executive Peer Tool (ExPT), which is a simplified version of the PAS presenting data from the IPEDS Data Feedback Report
3. The Dataset Cutting Tool (DCT), which allows users to create customized datasets of institution-level IPEDS data
4. College Navigator, which helps students and parents compare colleges on selected variables, including costs
5. The Data Analysis System (DAS), which allows users to generate analytical tables of percentages, means, or sums

A full description of these tools and their various capabilities, differences, and intricacies can be found at http://www.nces.ed.gov/IPEDS/tool_matrix/tool_matrix.asp. Obviously, numerous factors can be taken into account in using IPEDS data both for comparative purposes as well as for initially selecting peers.

Much of the information submitted to and deployed in IPEDS fuels comparison efforts by other organizations as well. For instance, many institutions complete the Common Data Set (CDS) annually in order to expeditiously share IPEDS type data with the guidebook publishers and magazines that publish college ratings and rankings. Many institutions make their CDS forms available through their institutional Website. When available, the CDS furnishes a wealth of information that can be used for comparative purposes. Data often made available through CDS forms may be slightly fresher, although certainly less comprehensive (to say nothing of having to track down CDS forms for individual institutions) than the data available through the various IPEDS data tools maintained by NCES. In addition, many of the publishers, such as Peterson's and *U.S. News and World Report*, make some of the data collected via the CDS and employed for ratings (and ranking) purposes available through their proprietary Websites, although a fee may be involved in accessing the data in a readily usable form for comparative purposes; see, for example, the premium service available from U.S. News (http://colleges.usnews.rankingsandreviews.com/usnews/edu/college/rankings/ranknatudoc_brief.php).

The Association of Governing Boards of Colleges and Universities (AGB) offers an online benchmarking service for its member institutions. Employing IPEDS data, such as those already described here, institutions subscribe to the service for an annual fee ($750 as of 2007-08). The service is aimed at institutions with tight resources and those wishing to produce readily accessible comparative reports. The focus of the analyses conducted by AGB is on supplying information for governing boards. The AGB Website (http://www.agb.org/wmspage.cfm?parm1=1113), reads in part:

> Boards and senior administrators need current data on a broad range of functions and concerns to use as benchmarks for their own institutions. Some institutions are in a better position than others to obtain comparative data, but if you can afford only a small institutional research enterprise—or if your institution wants to improve its capabilities—AGB's Benchmarking Service may be just right for you. . . . The service provides easy access to data for multiple years for hundreds of key performance variables. Select the data you need as well as the peer institutions you want for a custom comparison group. . . . The data and formats featured in these reports are appropriate for board use. They highlight the "big picture" financial and operational indicators boards want in order to fulfill their fiduciary and governance responsibilities.

Benchmarking services similar to those from AGB are also available through organizations such as the National Center for Higher Education Management Systems (NCHEMS). The data analyzed by NCHEMS are also drawn from the IPEDS database. NCHEMS' Comparison Group Selection Service (CGSS) "is designed to aid institutions in selecting a group of institutions which are similar in mission to be used in comparative data analyses" (http://www.nchems.org/services/infosvc/comparison.php_):

> CGSS consists of two primary components. The first is a large database containing indicator variables on each of more than 3,500 higher education institutions. . . . The indicator database contains variables covering institutional characteristics, faculty, finance, degrees awarded, enrollments, and other miscellaneous data. . . . The second component of the CGSS is a set of software programs designed to condense the 3,500+ institutions in the indicator database down to a useable list for a particular institution. This software uses a set of criteria supplied by the target institution to determine which institutions appear on the possible comparison institution list and their relative rankings within the list.

The Council of Independent Colleges (CIC), an organization designed to service the needs of small and midsize independent liberal arts colleges and universities, has a comparison group service as part of its Key Indicators Tool (KIT). Like the aforementioned benchmarking services, the comparison group KIT is available to CIC members for a fee. It too is based on IPEDS data. CIC focuses on helping institutions select the appropriate institutions for comparative analyses (http://www.cic.org/projects_services/infoservices/kit.asp).

Data for within-state comparisons certainly can be found by selecting appropriate schools for comparison groups; however, these data are also often available through state associations and advocacy groups such as the research center at the Association of Independent Colleges and Universities of Pennsylvania (AICUP). Similar to state associations, which obviously focus on data for institutions and issues of import at a state level, other organizations such as the Education Trust generate comparative data around topics of particular interest at the national level. For example, through its College Results Online Website, the Education Trust analyzes data and facilitates comparison of college graduation rates by race, ethnicity, and gender across four-year colleges and universities (http://www.collegeresults.org/). The Institute for College Access and Success (http://www.economicdiversity. org/index.php) offers a similar service analyzing institutional-level data on student income, race, ethnicity, and student loan usage.

The National Study of Instructional Costs and Productivity, commonly known as the Delaware Study, is "generally acknowledged as the 'tool of choice' for comparative analysis of faculty teaching loads, direct instructional cost, and separately budgeted scholarly activity, all at the level of the academic discipline. . . . It is a versatile and highly useful analytical tool for making management and policy decisions, whether at the level of the academic department, institution, state, or national level" (http://www.udel.edu/IR/cost/ welcome.html).

Surveys as a Source of Comparative Data

Most colleges and universities participate in, administer, or supply data to a variety of surveys every year. As noted already, these data collection activities include those mandated by governmental agencies and items such as the Common Data Set and surveys from various guidebooks and publishers. However, they also include data supplied to other organizations, such as the American Association of University Professors (AAUP), the College and University Personnel Association (CUPA), the Council for Aid to Education (CAE), and the National Association of College and University Business Officers (NACUBO) to name but a few. All of these efforts are sources of comparative data and should not be overlooked.

Similarly, our students, prospective students, faculty, and alumni are called on to complete a variety of individual surveys each year as well. The data generated from these surveys are also a source of comparison data, although generally not at the individual institutional level for institutions beyond one's own, but rather at an aggregate level sorted by institutional size, type, affiliation, level, location, and so on. These surveys include those conducted as part of the Cooperative Interinstitutional Research Program (CIRP) at the Higher Education Research Institute and the University of California Los Angeles, including an entering student survey, a survey at the end of the first year of college, an enrolled college student survey, and a faculty survey, and as well as those offered as part of the National Survey of Student Engagement (NSSE) effort out of Indiana University, Bloomington, which also includes surveys for entering students, enrolled students and faculty, and so forth. Data from these surveys can prove quite useful for benchmarking purposes and, though generally not available for direct institution-to-institution comparison, can often be accessed as part of consortial efforts in addition to being sorted by various factors such as affiliation, size, and type.

New Directions for Higher Education • DOI: 10.1002/he

Formal Data Sharing Consortia

Formal data sharing consortia serve as another means to access comparative data. However, unlike most of the efforts describe heretofore, data sharing consortia generally require active participation of institutions in
supplying, accessing, and using the data available through them. In addition, member schools are also often called on to lend some type of assistance
in administering, coordinating, guiding, and governing the activities of
the consortia. So, in many ways participating in a consortia is a good bit
more labor-intensive than accessing comparative data by way of other
avenues. However, data available through data sharing consortia are often
more useful than data from other sources in that the participating institutions generally help shape the agenda of the data sharing activity and help
decide what types of information are going to be collected, when they are
going to be collected, and how they are going to be shared. In addition, data
sharing consortia usually are formed by institutions that already share many
common attributes and serve as peers for one another for any number of
other activities.

Data sharing consortia come in a variety of shapes and sizes. As noted,
whole volumes have been dedicated to interinstitutional data exchange and
data sharing consortia. Shaman and Shapiro (1996) have examined the various dimensions of data sharing practice in an attempt to construct a typology of data sharing arrangements. They take into account eleven factors in
describing various data sharing consortia models: the formality of arrangements, primacy of purpose, control of the process, regularity of activity, the
scope of the information shared, the heterogeneity or homogeneity of participants, membership criteria, number of participants, openness of the
organization, the media of exchange, and the level of analysis provided.
They note that data are exchanged both with external organizations (such
as the government, the press, and other agencies) and within the educational
community. Data sharing consortia are an example of interinstitutional
exchange within the educational community. Illustrative exchanges are the
Higher Education Data Sharing Consortium (HEDS), the Consortium on
Financing Higher Education (COFHE), the Great Lakes Colleges Associa-
tion (GLCA), the Association of American Universities Data Exchange
(AAUDE), the Coalition of Christian Colleges and Universities (CCCU), the
Metropolitan University Group (MUG), the Southern University Group
(SUG), and the Committee on Institutional Cooperation (CIC) Data
Exchange.

Sapp (1996) notes participating in a data sharing organization can be
advantageous on many levels. Institutional benefits are access to comparison data from similar institutions, consortia-sponsored conferences, con-
sulting and other services, and efficiency. Benefits for individuals
representing institutions to consortia can be increased visibility and perceived value, better understanding of institutional issues, and developing

professional contacts. Such arrangements are not without their pitfalls, however: at the institutional level, there are costs in terms of time and money, missing data from key peer institutions, concerns with data collection methods and whether institutions can be compared, the potential reduction in the distinctiveness of institutions, and concerns about sensitive data. For the individual representatives to consortia, concerns are worry about resources, lack of institutional support for the data exchange activity, and so on. Potential problems notwithstanding, Fergerson (1996) notes that in addition to active sharing of specific data, access to e-mail distribution lists, listservs, and a network of colleagues is among the primary benefits of data sharing consortia.

Successful data sharing consortia generally follow a set of accepted ground rules. By their very nature, data exchanges are voluntary, participatory organizations. Consortia should define their membership and scope of activity carefully. Undoubtedly, their success will depend on consistent participation of members. In turn, participation in the exchange should be made as easy as possible, and the exchange should deliver a consistently high-quality product or service in a timely fashion and in a format that is useful to its members. Further, consortia should adhere to a strict policy limiting access to data for a given project to those institutions that have supplied the requisite data themselves. Structures must be put into place to address cost, resource, governance, and data use issues. With appropriate rules and structures in place, data sharing consortia can be extraordinarily successful (Trainer, 1996).

Conclusion

The ever-increasing level of access to the types and volumes of comparative data that are currently available to institutional researchers and administrators is unprecedented. Indeed, in this information and Internet age, one could easily argue that we are awash in data, some useful and some less so. The trick, then, is to know what types of benchmarking data are available, how to form appropriate and significant comparison groups, how to access needed data, and how to draw meaningful comparisons. Fortunately, the many and varied tools covered in this chapter are available to assist in this process.

References

Association of Governing Boards of Universities and Colleges. "Benchmarking Service," 2008. Retrieved Feb. 5, 2008, from http://www.agb.org/wmspage.cfm?parm1=1113.
Brinkman, P. T. (ed.). *Conducting Interinstitutional Comparisons.* New Directions for Institutional Research, no. 53. San Francisco: Jossey-Bass, 1987.
Carnegie Foundation for the Advancement of Teaching. "Classification Descriptions," 2007. Retrieved Feb. 5, 2008, from http://www.carnegiefoundation.org/classifications/index.asp.

Council of Independent Colleges. "Key Indicators Tool," 2007. Retrieved Feb. 5, 2008, http://www.cic.org/projects_services/infoservices/kit.asp.

Education Trust. "Welcome to College Results Online," 2007. Retrieved Feb. 5, 2008, from http://www.collegeresults.org/.

Fergerson, J. C. "Data Sharing and Keeping Pace with Changing Technologies." In J. F. Trainer (ed.), *Inter-Institutional Data Exchange: When to Do It, What to Look for, and How to Make It Work.* New Directions for Institutional Research, no. 89. San Francisco: Jossey-Bass, 1996.

Institute for College Access and Success. Economic Diversity of Colleges: College-Level Data for Researchers and the Public," 2006. Retrieved Feb. 5, 2008, from http://www.economicdiversity.org/index.php.

Knight, W. E. (ed.). *The Primer for Institutional Research.* Tallahassee, Fla.: Association for Institutional Research, 2003.

McLaughlin, G., and Howard, R. "Comparison Groups: Data and Decisions." Workshop presented at the Association for Institutional Research 45th Annual Forum, San Diego, June 2005.

National Center for Educational Statistics. "About IPEDS." U.S. Department of Education, 2007. Retrieved Feb. 5, 2008, from http://www.nces.ed.gov/IPEDS/about/.

National Center for Educational Statistics. "IPEDS Tool Finder." U.S. Department of Education, 2007. Retrieved Feb. 5, 2008, http://www.nces.ed.gov/IPEDS/tool_matrix/tool_matrix.asp.

National Center for Higher Education Management Systems. "Comparison Group Selection Service." National Center for Higher Education Management Systems, 2008. Retrieved Feb. 5, 2008, from http://www.nchems.org/services/infosvc/comparison.php.

Sapp, M. M. "Benefits and Potential Problems Associated with Effective Data-Sharing Consortia." In J. F. Trainer (ed.), *Inter-Institutional Data Exchange: When to Do It, What to Look for, and How to Make It Work.* New Directions for Institutional Research, no. 89. San Francisco: Jossey-Bass, 1996.

Shaman, S. M., and Shapiro, D. "Data Sharing Models." In J. F. Trainer (ed.), *Inter-Institutional Data Exchange: When to Do It, What to Look for, and How to Make It Work.* New Directions for Institutional Research, no. 89. San Francisco: Jossey-Bass, 1996.

Teeter, D. J. "The Politics of Comparing Data with Other Institutions." In J. W. Firnberg and W. F. Lasher (eds.), *The Politics and Pragmatics of Institutional Research.* New Directions for Institutional Research, no. 38. San Francisco: Jossey-Bass, 1983.

Teeter, D. J., and Brinkman, P. T. "Peer Institutions." In W. E. Knight (ed.), *The Primer for Institutional Research.* Tallahassee, Fla.: Association for Institutional Research, 2003.

Trainer, J. F. (ed.). *Inter-Institutional Data Exchange: When to Do It, What to Look for, and How to Make It Work.* New Directions for Institutional Research, no. 89. San Francisco: Jossey-Bass, 1996.

Trainer, J. F. "To Share and Share Alike: The Basic Ground Rules for Inter-institutional Data Sharing." In J. F. Trainer (ed.), *Inter-Institutional Data Exchange: When to Do It, What to Look for, and How to Make It Work.* New Directions for Institutional Research, no. 89. San Francisco: Jossey-Bass, 1996.

University of Delaware. "Welcome and Overview." *National Study of Instructional Costs and Productivity,* 2007. Retrieved Feb. 5, 2008, from http://www.udel.edu/IR/cost/welcome.html.

U.S. News & World Report. "America's Best Colleges 2008." Retrieved Feb. 5, 2008, from http://colleges.usnews.rankingsandreviews.com/usnews/edu/college/rankings/rankindex_brief.php.

JAMES F. TRAINER *is director of planning and assessment in the Office of Planning, Training, and Institutional Research (OPTIR) and special assistant to the vice president of academic affairs at Villanova University.*

NEW DIRECTIONS FOR HIGHER EDUCATION • DOI: 10.1002/he

3

Institutional Research has the potential to play an important role in assessment of student learning outcomes by lending leadership and assistance to departmental and institutional efforts.

The Role of Institutional Assessment in Assessing Student Learning Outcomes

Trudy H. Bers

There is a growing body of literature about assessment in higher education. Much of it is devoted to advocating the benefits of assessment, describing how assessment initiatives and programs might be organized within an institution, identifying key attributes of successful assessment projects (leadership, resources, faculty engagement), and explaining numerous assessment approaches and measures. Fewer publications present actual assessment results or detail how these results were used by a department or institution. This chapter has another purpose: identifying key ways in which institutional research offices furnish leadership or assistance in assessment. I limit my focus to assessment of student learning, an imperative that has been on the national agenda for more than a decade, especially in institutions accredited by the Higher Learning Commission (HLC) and the Southern Association of Colleges and Schools (SACS). Despite this, many colleges and universities still struggle with understanding assessment; engaging faculty in the process; generating internal resources in terms of money, energy, and time commitments; and presenting and using assessment results to improve learning and teaching.

Before continuing, I wish to acknowledge insights given to me by a number of my IR colleagues who have special expertise in assessing student-learning outcomes. They bring a combination of theoretical knowledge and practical experience to the conversation and have firsthand knowledge of the challenges inherent in assessing learning outcomes in the real world, engaging faculty who frequently view assessment as a burden imposed on them, and motivating students to take seriously work that often does not count in their grades.

NEW DIRECTIONS FOR HIGHER EDUCATION, no. 141, Spring 2008 © Wiley Periodicals, Inc.
Published online in Wiley InterScience (www.interscience.wiley.com) • DOI: 10.1002/he.291

Defining Learning Outcomes Assessment

What is assessment of student learning outcomes? At its most basic, assessment is determining whether students are learning what we intend for them to learn (Ewell, personal communication, Jan. 5, 2008). A more formal definition is from Ewell (2006): "Assessment comprises a set of systematic methods for collecting valid and reliable evidence of what students know and can do at various stages in their academic careers . . . governed by formal statements of student learning outcomes that are developed by a program's faculty or for the institution as a whole" (Ewell, 2006, p. 10).

Those who emphasize assessment for accountability want this information. Those whose focus is on quality improvement assert that assessment involves not just finding out whether students learned but also using assessment results to improve learning and teaching. Assessing student learning outcomes involves several steps, all of which should be part of the toolkit of institutional researchers even if, as we shall see below, the IR professional is not at the center of assessment within his or her institution. Assessment steps include:

- Clearly articulating the knowledge, skills, behaviors, and attitudes we expect students who successfully complete a segment of a course, an entire course, or a program to have and be able to demonstrate at the end of the learning experience.
- Identifying appropriate approaches to measure whether this learning has occurred and whether the student has achieved a specific threshold of performance to be considered "successful."
- Creating and following an assessment plan that not only specifies desired learning outcomes and assessment approaches but also identifies individuals responsible for administering and interpreting assessments, as well as reporting how results are communicated and how results were or will be used for institutional improvement. The timetable for assessment should also be part of the plan.

Assessment takes place at multiple levels: the classroom, course, program, general education, and institution. Classroom assessment, championed by Angelo and Cross (1993), is by definition private between the instructor and the students in the classroom. Intended to give the instructor immediate feedback about whether students understand material presented in the session and have questions or remain confused, classroom assessment is a powerful technique for improving teaching and learning. But classroom assessment does not satisfy departmental, institutional, or external demands for determining whether, regardless of the instructor, students meet learning objectives for a course, program, or institution. Because of this inherent limitation, institutional researchers and others charged with leading assessment activities may offer guidance in how to implement classroom assessments, but they should not consider these as substitutes for more broadly based learning outcomes assessments.

IR Brings Resources to the Assessment Table

Institutional researchers potentially bring many resources to the assessment table. Depending in part on the skills researchers have, these resources also vary according to placement of the IR office and assessment leadership within the institution, responsibilities assigned to the IR office, linkage among IR professionals and faculty, and the capacity of others at the institution to assess learning outcomes.

Among the most important strengths IR brings to assessment are researchers' knowledge of institutional student data and the ability to link institutional and assessment data from sources such as external tests, portfolio evaluations, and surveys. Many faculty, administrators, and staff members are simply unaware of the range of data that an institution typically stores about each student, let alone the operational definitions of data elements, issues of timing (when is enrollment in a course captured, for example), or the mechanics of extracting and manipulating data. Student information regularly maintained by an institution rarely contains direct assessment of learning, unless the institution has intentionally built learning assessment data into its information management system. Course grades, grade point averages, credits accumulated, and degrees or certificates awarded are generally considered indirect indicators of learning, although one could argue that if courses or programs possess clearly articulated learning objectives and students must demonstrate that they achieve these objectives in order to successfully complete the course or earn the award, then grades and degrees do reflect learning.

In addition to using institutional data, IR professionals often have the ability to link the institution's student unit records with external datasets—for example, statewide student datasets and unemployment insurance records. For assessment, there is still the question of whether behaviors identified through using external datasets (for example, transfer or working) are appropriate measures of learning. At best they are indirect indicators, but knowing whether students who leave an institution enrolled elsewhere, earned a degree, and entered and stayed in the labor force gives the institution important information even if it is not a direct measure of learning.

Another contribution institutional researchers make to assessment is methodological expertise in conducting research. For example, assessment novices may ask, "What percentage of students do we have to assess for our results to be valid?" IR can help them understanding sample sizes, confidence intervals and levels, the definition of validity, and (though it is not posed in this question) reliability. Researchers can also help assessors determine the statistics most appropriate for an analysis, the difference between causality and correlation or association, and the distinction between statistical and substantive significance. IR professionals can also help assessors design and test rubrics and compute interrater reliabilities when two or more evaluators assess a student's work.

IR professionals can offer critical assistance in helping faculty select assessment instruments, recognizing the practical realities and hidden costs as well as the potential benefits of using commercial and institutionally developed products. As Ewell (1985) notes, institutional researchers may actually conduct assessment research, especially when approaches such as tracking students or conducting alumni surveys are used.

Knowing how to present results meaningfully is another strength IR can bring to assessment, although I acknowledge that some institutional researchers are so intent on sharing every finding from research that they don't do as good a job as they should in considering and then highlighting what is meaningful in the results.

Because IR is not part of a specific academic department, it brings a neutral perspective to the assessment conversation. By focusing on the support of methodologically sound assessment techniques, appropriate use of data, and meaningful interpretation of assessment results, institutional researchers can deepen and enrich the value of assessment for the department and the institution. IR does not find itself in the awkward position of having to defend a department whose assessment results are poorer than desired, and it can help departments overcome defensiveness.

As Merkel and Litten (2007) note with respect to IR's role in sustainability, "IR is the purveyor of official institutional data for both internal and external users, and IR data have a high level of credibility" (p. 20). In the case of assessing learning outcomes, IR may not have this function, but the credibility of the IR office can be a critical asset in helping the institution report its assessment results, especially to external audiences.

IR professionals are accustomed to handling large amounts of data and information. As my colleague Joseph Hoey from the Savannah College of Art and Design noted, the "scale of doing assessment well at even a moderate-sized institution, and the necessity of collecting or acting as a central repository for a lot of assessment data, assessment plans, assessment action plans, etc., means that most IR shops engaged in this endeavor will absolutely have to leverage information technology to make it happen as well as to enable sustained, longitudinal assessment studies and evidence-based decision making to take place" (personal communication, Jan. 2008). I want to emphasize two of Hoey's points: the role of IR as a central repository for electronic and paper documents, and the value IR can bring to sustaining assessment processes and conducting longitudinal studies. These activities illustrate not just IR's content expertise but also the crucial role the IR office can play in managing the assessment enterprise.

IR professionals may be more attuned than many to the practical implications of research results. When assessments show that students aren't learning, the next questions ought to be why, what can be done to improve this, and how we will know that what we tried worked. In more abbreviated language, the question following assessment should be, Now what? IR can supply interpretations of results and management information to decision makers, and because IR assembles information from across the institution it may permit perspectives unavailable to a specific department or unit. Let me give an example.

A community college noticed that many students were habitually late to class, and that latecomers did not perform well. At first, faculty attributed this behavior to students' not caring, or not realizing they needed to be present for an entire session and not just part of one to acquire the knowledge and skills expected, or having priorities other than succeeding in school. Rather than assuming these suppositions were accurate, the institution decided to talk with students who were routinely late. The finding? The local bus, which many students depended on for transportation, was scheduled to arrive on campus a few minutes after the start of most classes. The remedy? The college learned that changing the start time of classes was easier than working with the bus company to revise its schedule. When the college adjusted the start time of classes, the problem of late-arriving students dissipated. The lesson for institutional research here is clear. In addition, using quantitative data from student information systems and other sources, the IR professional can design qualitative research projects that complement and augment quantitative studies. Although focus groups, in-depth interviews, and observations of student behavior may not furnish direct measures of learning, results from qualitative research can yield fruitful insights into why students learn or don't learn.

Though not always recognized or known within the institution, institutional researchers are remarkably collegial in sharing ideas, projects, and assistance with IR colleagues in other colleges and universities. The ethos of partnership therefore enables IR professionals to bring to their home institution good ideas and practices from elsewhere. Because institutions of all types are charged with assessing student learning outcomes, the IR culture of collaboration opens a wealth of external learning opportunities to those assessing student learning outcomes within an institution. Moreover, because the literature about assessment contains relatively little with respect to what doesn't work or what assessment findings actually were and how they were used, informal exchange of information among IR colleagues brings rich insights to augment published information.

Impediments to IR Success in the Institutional Assessment Arena

Absence from the table is the most serious and obvious barrier affecting IR's ability to contribute to assessing student learning outcomes. This absence may be due to a variety of factors. One is an organizational structure that intentionally or unintentionally fails to recognize that assessment is a form of applied research, and institutional research *is* applied research. A second is failure of IR professionals to network and connect with faculty and others charged with doing assessment, leading to a situation where they either don't recognize or (uncomfortable as this is to admit) may be put off by IR. A third is an overemphasis on faculty "owning" assessment, creating a monopolistic situation where no one but faculty are perceived as legitimate stakeholders in assessment. A fourth factor is an IR agenda that is crowded with projects that are, or seem to be, of greater importance than assessment; this factor is especially powerful if the institution perceives that assessment is taking place anyway and doesn't need IR involvement. Finally, IR may not have a place at the table because of an institutional perception that IR's role is simply that of counting and reporting rather than engaging in research and helping to inform and implement assessments.

IR professionals must also examine their own behavior to gauge whether they are jeopardizing their own success. For example, some in IR have a propensity to seek perfect data and accuracy, carrying numbers to multiple decimals when simple percentages tell the story and filling reports with arcane methodological details better presented in an appendix or agendas that don't allow space for assessment.

Another barrier occurs if IR professionals are perceived as unfamiliar with the realities of classroom instruction, assessing student performance, and creating learning outcome objectives at the course or program level. Though no guarantee that the individual will have such experience, it is helpful if the institutional researcher has also had experience as a faculty member, even if as an adjunct.

This may seem a contradiction to the point made earlier about the IR culture encouraging sharing of information, but I would be remiss if I didn't note that comparing student learning outcomes across institutions, as distinct from sharing approaches for assessing this learning, has not been high on the IR agenda. Though it is too soon to know the full impact of the Spellings Commission's recommendations on assessment, the final report clearly states that "postsecondary education institutions should measure and report meaningful student learning outcomes" (U.S. Department of Education, 2006, p. 24). The report goes on to argue that accreditation agencies should revise their standards to allow "comparisons among institutions regarding learning outcomes" (p. 25). As the national debate about accreditation standards and assessment continues, it is likely that institutions will voluntarily or under mandate make learning outcomes evidence more public and comparable. It is also likely that IR will play a central role in doing so at many institutions.

The Association for Institutional Research and Assessment

No discussion of the role of IR in assessment would be complete without describing the activities of the Association for Institutional Research (AIR) in this arena. AIR is the primary professional organization for institutional researchers. When assessment rose to prominence in the higher education landscape in the late 1980s, the American Association for Higher Education (AAHE) took the lead in organizing national assessment forums about assessing student learning. There was some discussion within AIR about taking a more proactive role in offering professional development on the topic of assessment, but the organization did not assertively pursue this agenda. However, the number of proposals about assessment submitted for the AIR National Forum continued to increase. Interest in assessment was also evident at regional and state AIR meetings.

AAHE went out of existence in 2005, and though there are a variety of state, regional, and national meetings devoted wholly or in substantial part to assessment, no group has been recognized as the assessment leader comparable to the visibility AAHE had during the early years of this century. At the same time, the demand for assessment has continued to grow, spawned in part by calls for accountability and in part by the recognition among some institutional leaders that assessment was of paramount importance for institutional improvement.

AIR has stepped up its investment in assessment for at least three reasons: (1) the void in national organizational leadership for assessment since the demise of AAHE, (2) continuing pressure on institutions to conduct and report on the assessment of student learning, and (3) recognition of the central role IR could and should play in assessment because of the knowledge and skills of IR professionals and the unique position of IR offices within institutions. Today, AIR's Website notes that "the Association for Institutional Research (AIR), one of the first organizations to promote the measurement of student learning and the use of student assessment research to increase the effectiveness of higher education, offers its members a wide variety of assessment-related programs and resources." The *Professional File*, a quarterly publication that is a synthesis of key issues about a topic, that introduces research process or models, and that shares practical information about a research topic of interest across a spectrum of institutions, includes a number of issues devoted to assessment. *IR Applications*, a newer, Web-based publication that presents articles focused on application of advanced and specialized methodologies, has also presented issues devoted to assessment. *New Directions in Institutional Research*, a quarterly sourcebook published by Jossey-Bass under the sponsorship and policies of AIR, has focused on assessment in several issues and contains chapters related to assessment in others (for example, Dalton, Russell, and Kline, 2004; Ewell, 1985; Voorhees, 2001). Beginning in 2008, the *New Directions* series also includes a supplemental issue on assessment. The annual forum continues to include a range of workshops and presentations about assessment. Recently the association launched a new book series focusing on assessment within the disciplines, and in 2008 it initiated a five-day residential institute on assessment.

AIR's accelerated activity regarding assessment demonstrates the IR profession's recognition that (1) assessment is an important arena for IR professionals, (2) continuing professional development is needed, and (3) assessment will remain high on the national applied research agenda for higher education.

Institutional Responsibility for Assessment

The preceding discussion emphasizes the many contributions institutional research can make to assessment of student learning. Obviously, there are many. A related question, one not touched on above, is whether IR should be the primary office responsible for coordinating assessment. With resounding certainty, my response is, "It depends." Ideally, assessment should be centered in an office directly associated with the teaching-learning process, probably academic affairs. Absent faculty involvement, assessing student learning will be weak and tangential to the business of learning, teaching, and institutional improvement. However, a number of contingencies affect the best assignment of assessment responsibility for an institution.

One contingency is whether the institution has an institutional effectiveness office, and whether this office is also responsible for institutional research or for assessing learning outcomes. In large organizations, there may be sufficient staff and work to support several offices, each of which has research or programmatic responsibilities related to the broad concepts of quality and accountability. In smaller colleges, these responsibilities may need to be combined into a single office.

A second contingency is institutional history and professional talent, which I put together because often the skills and interests of a long-time employee have as much to do with shaping the structure of a college as do organizational theories or management models. Put another way, there is no single right way of organizing for assessment. What works at one institution may be totally inappropriate at another.

Another contingency is the association and timing of accreditation or other significant institutional imperatives and assessment. If the college has a sense of urgency about assessment because of an impending accreditation review, application for a Baldrige or similar award, or involvement in initiatives related to assessment such as the Foundations of Excellence or Achieving the Dream, then IR may be perceived as more essential than during periods when assessment is less visible externally.

Conclusion

It is evident from this discussion that institutional research has an important role to play in assessing student-learning outcomes, but also that the extent to which IR is involved in assessment varies across colleges and universities. It seems clear that assessing and reporting on student learning will

NEW DIRECTIONS FOR HIGHER EDUCATION • DOI: 10.1002/he

be of continuing importance as institutions realize the centrality of student learning to fulfilling their mission and to meeting stakeholder expectations that investments in higher education do in fact result in students acquiring knowledge, skills, attitudes, and behaviors aligned with course and program objectives. It is also discouraging that nearly two decades after assessment became prominent on the national agenda and particularly targeted by some regional accrediting agencies, so many institutions continue to struggle with convincing faculty that assessment matters and with institutionalizing assessment as part and parcel of how the organization works. Institutional research can help, but it cannot meet assessment expectations on its own.

References

Angelo, T. A., and Cross, K. P. *Classroom Assessment Techniques: A Handbook for College Teachers* (2nd ed.). San Francisco: Jossey-Bass, 1993.

Dalton, J. D., Russell, T .R., and Kline, S. (eds.). *Assessing Character Outcomes in College.* New Directions for Institutional Research, no. 122. San Francisco: Jossey-Bass, 2004.

Ewell, P. T. (ed.). *Assessing Educational Outcomes.* New Directions for Institutional Research, no. 47. San Francisco: Jossey-Bass, 1985.

Ewell, P. T. *Making the Grade: How Boards Can Ensure Academic Quality.* Washington, D.C.: Association of Governing Boards of Colleges and Universities, 2006.

Merkel, J., and Litten, L. H. "The Sustainability Challenge." In L. H. Litten and D. G. Terkla (eds.), *Advancing Sustainability in Higher Education: Measuring What Matters—Competency-Based Learning Models in Higher Education.* New Directions for Institutional Research, no. 134. San Francisco: Jossey-Bass, 2007.

U.S. Department of Education. *A Test of Leadership: Charting the Future of U.S. Higher Education.* Washington, D.C., 2006. (http://www.ed.gov/about/bdscomm/list/hiedfuture/reports/pre-pub-report.pdf).

Voorhees, R. (ed.). *Measuring What Matters: Competency-Based Learning Models in Higher Education.* New Directions for Institutional Research, no. 110. San Francisco: Jossey-Bass, 2001.

TRUDY H. BERS *is executive director, research, curriculum, and planning, at Oakton Community College.*

NEW DIRECTIONS FOR HIGHER EDUCATION • DOI: 10.1002/he

4

Understanding faculty workload is critical in assessing and describing institutional effectiveness. The Delaware Study of Instructional Costs and Productivity is one example.

The Role of Institutional Research in Understanding and Describing Faculty Work

Michael F. Middaugh, Heather A. Kelly, Allison M. Walters

The current landscape of higher education requires those in academe to be accountable to an array of constituents. With students, parents, and government seeking proof of a return on their investment and efficient management of fiscal and human resources, it is essential to have access to appropriate and useful data when researching the operation of an institution and its faculty.

Given the central role of the faculty and their involvement with students in and outside the classroom, it is critical to understand faculty work in order to assess institutional effectiveness. Since the late 1980s, data about faculty work have been reported and studied by three prominent national efforts. The first, the National Study of Postsecondary Faculty (NSOPF), was conducted by the National Center for Education Statistics (NCES) in 1988, 1993, 1999, and 2004 (National Center for Education Statistics [NCES], n.d.). The study samples institutional faculty and other instructional staff, asking questions about how faculty spend their time, how many courses they teach in a given term, and the types of research and service activities in which they engage. NSOPF also asks questions regarding faculty demographics, academic background, compensation, and their feelings of institutional support.

The resulting data furnished by NSOPF on the NCES Website are displayed by institution type (public research, public two-year, and so on) and general program area (business, education, and the like). According to the Website, NSOPF data are meant for use by higher education researchers,

NEW DIRECTIONS FOR HIGHER EDUCATION, no. 141, Spring 2008 © Wiley Periodicals, Inc.
Published online in Wiley InterScience (www.interscience.wiley.com) • DOI: 10.1002/he.292

planners, and policy makers. Because of the large samples and high response rates, the data are helpful in gaining a general understanding of faculty work in American higher education over time. The reports display data about what faculty are doing—how many hours per week they spend teaching and the percentage of time they spend on teaching, research, and service activities.

Though these data can assist in the understanding of the nature of faculty work at various types of institutions and within disciplinary areas, the information is too general to support internal management decisions on a given campus. The data results are based only on self-reported data, begging the question: how can these be verified? The data are also based on general terms of faculty and disciplinary area. In particular, the data are not delineated by level or type of faculty other than full-time or part-time instructional faculty/staff. The data only discuss faculty work in general terms of hours per week, student contact hours, percent of time in teaching, research, and service, and number and types of publications. While NSOPF data can be analyzed for relationships between faculty work and compensation and satisfaction yielding descriptive and valuable results, the data lack sufficient detail for making meaningful comparisons between departments or institutions.

The second, the Higher Education Research Institute (HERI) Faculty Survey, initiated its triennial administration series in 1989 and is conducting its tenth survey in the series in 2007-08 (Higher Education Research Institute [HERI], 2007). Similar to NSOPF, the HERI Faculty Survey asks an institution's faculty questions about their workload and teaching activities (number of courses taught in a term and students enrolled, number of hours per week spent on teaching and a variety of other activities, and so forth), as well as satisfaction and compensation. The HERI Faculty Survey also asks faculty about their goals for general education and other student outcomes, as well as their engagement with undergraduates in teaching, research, and service.

The HERI Faculty Survey gives each participating institution a results profile, with data grouped by the institution as a whole as well as by general programmatic areas. Participants also receive a data profile of norms from a set of similar institutions by type, control, and selectivity. This survey adds value to an institution's internal management decisions because it is an opportunity to conduct comparator analyses to similar institutions, as well as to the national norm data published in HERI's *The American College Teacher.* In addition, the survey includes questions on faculty engagement with students and development of teaching toward student learning outcomes, which can assist institutional planning and effectiveness as well as improve faculty productivity.

Though this information is valuable, the HERI Faculty Survey shares some of the same limitations as NSOPF. In particular, the results are based on self-reported data and the faculty are still reported in a general manner. Self-reported data usually encounter credibility problems when shared with anyone outside of academe, whether state or federal government, parents, or local industry. It is also important to note that the HERI Faculty Survey bases its normative data only on full-time undergraduate faculty, which does not furnish a complete picture when examining departments at institutions around the country where faculty are engaged in graduate-level teaching and research.

The third, the Faculty Survey of Student Engagement (FSSE), administered since 2003 by the Center for Postsecondary Research at Indiana University Bloomington, measures faculty opinions on the extent to which students engage in their education (Center for Postsecondary Research, 2008). FSSE results contain faculty profile data and time spent on teaching, research, and service activities comparable to NSOPF and the HERI Faculty Survey. Like the National Survey of Student Engagement (NSSE), FSSE's primary focus is student engagement; therefore it is a unique method of comparison to NSSE results allowing an institution to examine differences and identify areas of growth in students' experiences with faculty. FSSE results pertaining to faculty work, however, share similar shortcomings with NSOPF and the HERI Faculty Survey. In particular, the data are self-reported, focus only on undergraduate teaching and learning, and do not yield results at the academic discipline level of analysis.

These three studies offer valuable information for understanding what faculty do; however, the limitations of NSOPF, the HERI Faculty Survey, and FSSE point to additional areas worth studying to describe faculty work. Institutional researchers need to use measurements that generate more particular and narrower results within the area of faculty workload and productivity if we are to meet the managerial needs of our institutional administrators and financial planners.

Appropriate Focus for Researching Faculty Work

In 2003, the Office of Institutional Research and Planning at the University of Delaware received a contract from the National Center for Education Statistics (NCES) to examine factors that contribute to increases in the cost of higher education at four-year institutions in the United States. The University of Delaware was selected because the Office of Institutional Research and Planning has been the analytical center for the Delaware Study of Instructional Costs and Productivity since 1992. The Delaware Study annually collects detailed information on faculty teaching loads, instructional costs, and externally funded scholarship, all at the academic discipline level of analysis. Since its inception, more than five hundred institutions have participated in the Delaware Study. This discussion summarizes that work (Middaugh, Graham, and Shahid, 2003).

In approaching analysis of instructional costs, we used data from the 1998, 2000, and 2001 Delaware Study data collection cycles. Data collection was limited in scope in 1999, because the University of Delaware was testing a secure Web server for collection, analysis, and dissemination of Delaware Study data. Using appropriate statistical tools, the data were examined to identify factors that explain the variation in instructional expenditures across four-year institutions participating in the study. Most of the variation (in excess of 80 percent) is explained by the disciplines that constitute the curriculum at a given institution. A secondary factor affecting cost is the institution's 1995 Carnegie classification (research, doctoral, comprehensive, or baccalaureate).

Disciplines exerting such a strong influence on cost can best be seen by looking at the 2001 Delaware Study data through two lenses. Consider five disciplines typically found at four-year institutions: chemistry, English, foreign languages, mechanical engineering, and sociology. Figure 4.1 displays direct instructional expense per student credit hour taught, looking at variation in the mean cost by Carnegie classification within each discipline.

Although cost varies within each discipline according to Carnegie classification, the differences from high to low are not that large: $83 in chemistry, $28 in English, $71 in foreign languages, $63 in mechanical engineering, and $38 in sociology.

However, when we examine the difference between cost per credit hour among the five disciplines within each of the four Carnegie classifications, the results are far more dramatic. The difference between the most costly and least costly discipline at research universities is $255, for doctoral universities $210, comprehensive institutions $242, and baccalaureate institutions $110. Figure 4.2 displays these differences.

Figure 4.1. Direct Instructional Expense per Student Credit Hour Taught: Institution Type Within Discipline (Academic Year 2001)

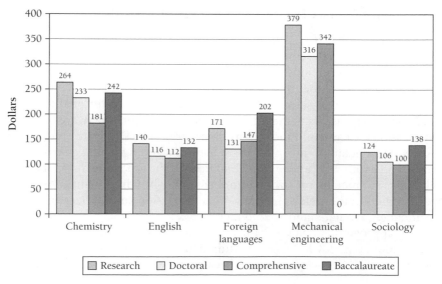

Figure 4.2. Direct Instructional Expense per Student Credit Hour Taught: Discipline Within Institution Type (Academic Year 2001)

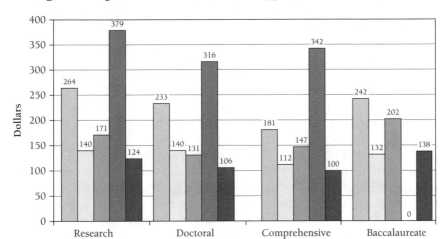

With the variation in direct instructional expenditures so highly dependent on the curricular mix of disciplines at an institution, it is important to understand the factors within those disciplines that have an impact on expenditures. Again using Delaware Study data and appropriate statistical tools, it was determined that 60–75 percent of the variation in cost within a discipline across institutions is associated with specific cost factors:

- The volume of teaching activity, measured in student credit hours taught, is a major factor in instructional expense. The higher the number of credit hours taught, the lower the cost.
- Department size, measured in terms of the total number of faculty, is a strong cost indicator. The larger the department, the higher the expense.
- The proportion of faculty who hold tenure is a cost factor. As one might expect, the higher the tenure rate, the higher the cost.
- The presence of graduate instruction within a discipline is a cost factor, but it is much more weakly associated with expense than with the volume of teaching, department size, and tenure rate.

If one simply looked at these data alone, the temptation would be to arrive at a draconian policy that increased the volume of teaching activity, reduced the size of academic departments, and eliminated tenure. Teaching activity is certainly important, but faculty engage in an array of other activities that support the mission of a college or university. The foregoing NCES analysis (Middaugh, Graham, and Shahid, 2003) suggests that, if there is to be a discussion of faculty work, it should be within the context of the academic discipline. The remainder of this chapter focuses on how institutional research in general, and the Delaware Study of Instructional Costs and Productivity in particular, can inform that discussion.

Understanding Faculty Productivity: Teaching Loads and Costs

Direct expenditures for instruction make up 50–75 percent of the operating budget at most four-year institutions in the United States (Middaugh, 2001). With costs at this magnitude, it is fair to seek analytical strategies that describe return on investment. The University of Delaware developed such strategies in the late 1980s when confronted with a regional economic recession that severely curtailed state assistance to the institution. A series of budget support metrics were developed that enable detailed examination of academic department teaching loads, instructional costs, and externally funded scholarly activity. The evolution of these budget support metrics is described in detail in the book *Understanding Faculty Productivity: Standards and Benchmarks for Colleges and Universities* (Middaugh, 2001). Among the indicators that were developed:

- Total student credit hours taught per FTE faculty
- Undergraduate student credit hours taught per FTE faculty
- Graduate student credit hours taught per FTE faculty
- FTE students taught per FTE faculty
- Total direct instructional expense per student credit hour taught
- Total direct instructional expense per FTE student taught
- Total externally funded research and service per FTE tenured–tenure track faculty

These measures enabled comparisons between and among disciplines with pedagogical affinity, such as history compared to political science, physics compared to chemistry, studio art compared to music performance, and so on. The objective was to study the measures over time and, where productivity in a department was consistently lower and costs higher than in comparable units, to determine whether qualitative dimensions of departmental activity could offset those measures. Where high quality was not apparent, the unit became a candidate for resource reallocation. The budget support metrics encouraged academic units to closely examine the extent to which they were effectively and efficiently using human and fiscal resources in support of the instructional function.

As useful as these interdepartmental comparisons within the university were in assessing relative productivity and cost, senior administration encouraged the Office of Institutional Research and Planning to develop cross-institutional comparisons that would draw on data from other institutions.

NEW DIRECTIONS FOR HIGHER EDUCATION • DOI: 10.1002/he

From this directive, the Delaware Study of Instructional Costs and Productivity was born.

The Delaware Study began in 1992 with an initial participant pool of just under one hundred four-year institutions. The number of schools participating in the study since its inception is now more than five hundred. The Delaware Study data collection instrumentation and methodology have evolved into what is now viewed as a state-of-the-art approach to collecting detailed information on faculty teaching loads, instructional costs, and externally funded scholarship.

The measures developed from the Delaware Study data are conceptually similar to the University of Delaware budget support metrics described earlier, but they produce considerably more information. For example, teaching activity is examined for four discrete categories of faculty. Tenured and tenure eligible faculty are examined, but so too are what are referred to as "other regular faculty." These typically are full-time faculty on recurring contracts who are hired primarily to teach, with no expectation of scholarship or service and with no possibility of academic tenure. This category of faculty has shown rapid growth over the past decade. The teaching activity of supplemental faculty (adjunct faculty, administrators teaching courses) and graduate teaching assistants is also examined. Within each category of faculty, data are collected for lower- and upper-division undergraduate and graduate instruction in both regularly scheduled classes and independent study.

Data are also collected for regularly scheduled course sections that may carry zero credit, such as recitation, discussion, and laboratory sections that support the credit-bearing portion of a course, all consuming instructional resources. Thus the full range of faculty instructional activity is captured. The budget support measures on externally funded scholarship are methodologically replicated in the Delaware Study to furnish data on funded research and service activity per FTE tenured and tenure track faculty.

How are Delaware Study data typically used? At the University of Delaware, the practice is to share data with all of the deans and department chairs in the seven colleges. The data that all participating institutions receive from the Delaware Study are detailed and voluminous; this sort of information appeals to institutional researchers, but the data tables are not suitable for sharing with busy administrators. The Office of Institutional Research and Planning met with the provost, deans, and department chairs and the decision was made to focus on tenured and tenure track faculty, because their salaries are significant drivers of instructional expense and they can be viewed as "fixed costs" once tenure is granted. Rather than complex data tables, academic leadership is given a single page for each academic discipline, with six charts detailing:

1. Undergraduate student credit hours taught per FTE tenured–tenure track faculty
2. Total student credit hours taught per FTE tenured–tenure track faculty

New Directions for Higher Education • DOI: 10.1002/he

3. Total class sections taught per FTE tenured–tenure track faculty
4. Total student credit hours taught per FTE faculty, all categories combined
5. Total direct instructional expense per student credit hour taught
6. Total separately budgeted research and service expenditures per FTE tenured–tenure track faculty

Figure 4.3 displays the actual departmental profile for a science unit at the University of Delaware, as it appeared in 2001. A graph compares the University of Delaware measure for the respective variable with the national benchmark for research universities participating in the Delaware Study in each year under examination. It is evident that from 1994 through 1997 the volume of teaching at the University of Delaware, as measured in terms of student credit hours taught, is generally comparable to the national benchmark. However, during the same years the university measure for externally funded research and service activity was well below the national benchmark.

In 1995, a new department chair was hired with the mandate that research productivity must increase. The chair assured that this was achievable, but only if tenured and tenure-eligible faculty received release time to prepare grant proposals and actually do the research once the grants were received. This was agreed to; the decline in student credit hours taught by tenured and tenure track faculty from 1997 through 1999 in the first two graphs in Figure 4.3 was a *planned* decline. The teaching of courses that heretofore had been done by tenured–tenure track faculty was shifted to the category of faculty referred to earlier as "other regular faculty" (recurring, full-time, nontenurable faculty hired primarily to teach). Delaware Study data were used to achieve a restructuring of departmental faculty work in a fashion more consistent with the university mission.

The general guideline for using Delaware Study data at the University of Delaware is that the data from any given year will not be used to reward or penalize a department. Rather, data are to be examined over time as a tool of inquiry for asking why University of Delaware measures are similar to or different from the national benchmarks, with an eye toward programmatic quality as an essential part of the answer. Because the Delaware Study data just described focus largely on quantitative measures of faculty teaching and research activity, it is imperative to have some mechanism for accounting for other types of faculty work. Indeed, what faculty do outside the classroom and laboratory can have a profound impact on the volume of teaching and sponsored research activity within a given academic unit.

Understanding Faculty Productivity: Out-of-Classroom Faculty Activity

Within academe, it is understood that faculty have three primary responsibilities: teaching, scholarly activity, and service. This notion has been confirmed over time through administration of NSOPF and the HERI Faculty

NEW DIRECTIONS FOR HIGHER EDUCATION • DOI: 10.1002/he

Figure 4.3. Science Department

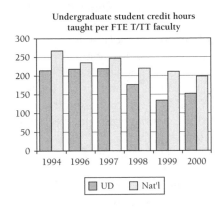

Undergraduate student credit hours taught per FTE T/TT faculty

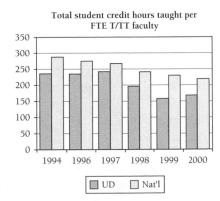

Total student credit hours taught per FTE T/TT faculty

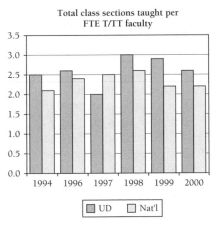

Total class sections taught per FTE T/TT faculty

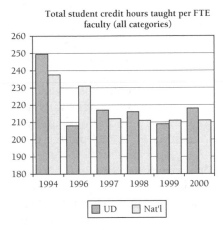

Total student credit hours taught per FTE faculty (all categories)

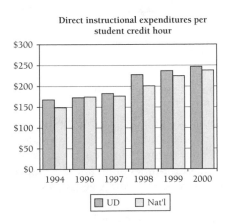

Direct instructional expenditures per student credit hour

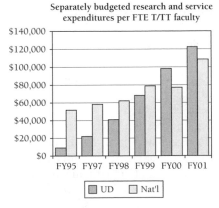

Separately budgeted research and service expenditures per FTE T/TT faculty

Survey. However, the perception outside academe is that faculty have one primary responsibility: to teach students. This is further compounded by NSOPF data. According to the 2003 NSOPF, full-time faculty at four-year institutions report they work approximately fifty-four hours per week (Cataldi, Bradburn, Fahimi, and Zimbler, 2005). These data indicate how many hours per week faculty work, but how do faculty members actually spend their time? In additional 2003 NSOPF data, full-time instructional faculty and staff at four-year institutions report they spend more than half (58 percent) of their time on teaching activities, which includes approximately nine hours per week in the classroom; 22 percent of their time on research activities; and 21 percent of their time on administrative and other activities (Cataldi, Bradburn, Fahimi, and Zimbler, 2005). One might say the NSOPF data accurately reflect faculty responsibilities in order of priority: teaching, research, and service.

Although NSOPF data yield information on how faculty spend their time, a question remains: "Are faculty being productive with their time?" A number of parties would be interested in the answer, among them those who fund higher education (state legislatures, federal government, and students and parents), higher education trustees and administrators, and faculty themselves.

NSOPF, the HERI Faculty Survey, and FSSE generate valuable information on how faculty spend their time; however, this information describes input measures. It is imperative, with increased calls for accountability in academe, that output measures and the actual products of faculty activity be captured. If faculty productivity is to be discussed and understood, output measures that fully and adequately describe the broad spectrum of faculty activity, as well as the associated products, need to be articulated. Taking a closer look at the teaching load and cost portion of the Delaware Study shows that this study suffers from an absence of contextual information that describes what faculty do when they are not in the classroom—activity that may directly affect the volume of teaching and associated instructional expenditures.

Realizing the absence of this contextual information, the University of Delaware applied for and was awarded a three-year grant from the Fund for the Improvement of Postsecondary Education (FIPSE) in 2001, to expand the scope of the Delaware Study to address out-of-classroom dimensions of faculty activity. The primary intent of the Out-of-Classroom Faculty Activity Study is to help alleviate misunderstandings about faculty work by furnishing information to discuss what faculty actually do, how much they do, and the associated products. DeGeorge (1997) has suggested that accountability measures of faculty productivity must be easy to understand and developed by faculty and higher education administration. Specifically, DeGeorge states:

> In the absence of proper evaluations of the development of knowledge, legislatures, boards of directors, and the general citizenry often seek measures they understand, and they seek quantitative measures with which they are familiar, whether or not such measures are proper instruments for measuring

whether the institution is fulfilling its mission, and how well it is doing so. The easiest measure is the number of students or credit hours taught or the number of degrees awarded. . . . Since the faculty and the administration of the university are the experts in what they do and teach, it is they who should suggest, develop, and defend instruments and means of providing account-ability [p. 66].

The Delaware Study took DeGeorge's belief to heart. Similar to the teaching load and cost portion of the Delaware Study, an advisory committee was established to bring together experts in assessing faculty activity and research design. The committee comprised faculty members, institutional researchers, university system administrators, university trustees, and representatives from higher education associations. The intent was to bring together the most well-informed individuals to define and refine the data collection instrumentation and methodology. The Out-of-Classroom Faculty Activity Study instrument currently consists of forty-two variables relating to teaching, scholarship, and service. These are the variables:

1. Separate course preparations developed by faculty
2. Existing courses where faculty have developed or redesigned the pedagogy or curriculum
3. New courses faculty have created and approved for delivery
4. New courses faculty have created to be delivered fully or primarily online
5. Undergraduate academic advisees formally assigned to faculty
6. Graduate academic advisees formally assigned to faculty
7. Thesis or dissertation committees where faculty served as chairperson
8. Thesis or dissertation committees where faculty served in a nonchairing role
9. Undergraduate senior theses that faculty have supervised
10. Students taught individually in independent or directed studies
11. Undergraduate students formally engaged in research with a faculty mentor
12. Graduate students formally engaged in noncredit research with a faculty mentor
13. Number of clinical, practicum, internship students, and students in cooperative and service learning education programs
14. Students (undergraduate or graduate) who have co-authored a journal article or book chapter with a faculty mentor
15. Students (undergraduate or graduate) who have co-presented a paper at a professional meeting with a faculty mentor
16. Number of assessment projects or separate assignments for purpose of program evaluation
17. Institution-sanctioned professional development activities related to teaching efforts

18. Print or electronic refereed journal articles, book chapters, or creative works
19. Print or electronic nonrefereed journal articles, book chapters, or creative works
20. Single-author or joint-author books or monographs
21. Manuscripts submitted to publishers
22. Edited books, collections, or monographs
23. Review of prepublication books, journal articles, and chapters
24. Grant proposals reviewed by faculty related to field of expertise
25. Editorial positions
26. Juried shows, commissioned performances, creative readings, or competitive exhibitions
27. Nonjuried shows, commissioned performances, creative readings, or competitive exhibitions
28. Digital programs or applications designed by faculty related to field of expertise
29. Provisional or issued patents based on faculty products
30. Faculty works in progress
31. Formal presentations made at state, regional, national, and international professional meetings
32. External and internal grant, contract, and scholarly fellowship proposals
33. External grants, contracts, and scholarly fellowships formally awarded
34. Total dollar value for externally funded grants, contracts, and scholarly fellowships
35. Internal grants and contracts formally awarded
36. Total dollar value for internal grants and contracts
37. Continuing external and internal grants, contracts, and scholarly fellowships
38. Institution-sanctioned professional development activities related to scholarship
39. Faculty activities related to institutional service
40. Faculty extension and outreach activities related to field of expertise
41. Faculty activities related to recognized or visible service to profession
42. Leadership positions in a professional association

The Out-of-Classroom Faculty Activity Study has some associated challenges. A major challenge for the study is that out-of-classroom faculty activity data typically do not reside in a central database on campus. This type of information is typically collected by way of faculty evaluations and locked away in a department chair's file cabinet. Another challenge is motivating faculty to participate in the study in order to increase the response rate. The data are presented as a ratio per FTE tenured and tenure-track faculty respondents, so a high response rate is essential to ensure that a department's out-of-classroom faculty activity is accurately represented.

NEW DIRECTIONS FOR HIGHER EDUCATION • DOI: 10.1002/he

Additional elements impede data collection for the Out-of-Classroom Faculty Activity Study. For one, this type of data may appear threatening to individual faculty members because the variables collected in this study are some of the same ones used to make promotion and tenure decisions. In addition, some faculty will be disgruntled because they are asked numerous times to supply activity data during a given year. One of the biggest challenges is gaining department chair and faculty buy-in because they may not have control over how the data is used. For this reason, department chairs and faculty must understand why this type of information is needed and how the information will be employed. Department chairs and faculty gain this understanding through extensive conversation with the Office of Institutional Research. Moreover, the support of senior administrators is critical and facilitates the data collection process.

The FIPSE grant supported the writing of two briefing papers that reviewed institutions having exemplary data collection practices with regard to out-of-classroom faculty activity. The first briefing paper reviewed institutions with exemplary *electronic* data collection practices. This briefing paper, "A Study of Exemplary Practices in Collection of Data on Out-of-Classroom Faculty Activity," was printed in July 2004 (http://www.udel.edu/IR/focs/DEStudyBrief.pdf). The institutions reviewed were Binghamton University, Clemson University, and Montana State University. These are fairly large, complex public institutions that have the resources to establish a Web-based data collection tool to facilitate collection and analysis of faculty activity data.

The second briefing paper reviewed institutions with exemplary *traditional* data collection practices. This briefing paper, "A Study of Exemplary Practices in Collection of Data on Out-of-Classroom Faculty Activity: Part II," was printed in September 2005 (http://www.udel.edu/IR/focs/DEStudyBrief2.pdf). The institutions reviewed were Ohio Northern University, Rider University, Southeastern Louisiana University, and the University of West Florida. These are smaller, public and private baccalaureate and comprehensive institutions. These institutions lacked the resources to establish a Web-based data collection tool for faculty activity so they used more traditional data collection and analytical processes. The key to their success was that they all secured widespread campus support for the Out-of-Classroom Faculty Activity Study.

Similar to the teaching load and cost portion of the Delaware Study, the Out-of-Classroom Faculty Activity Study data allow participating institutions to benchmark the relevant information by Carnegie classification or highest degree offered, all at the discipline level of analysis. Let's take a look at the Out-of-Classroom Faculty Activity Study median analysis results for a science department by Carnegie classification (Figure 4.4). As expected, with respect to teaching baccalaureate institutions do not show any evidence of graduate research or graduate advisees. There is a noticeable downward trend from baccalaureate to research institutions with regard to redesigning

Figure 4.4. Activities Related to Teaching, Scholarship, and Service per FTE T/TT Faculty

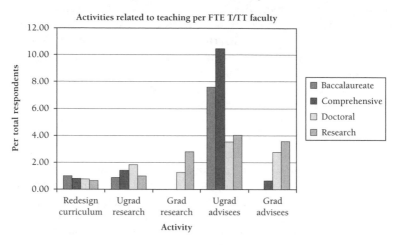

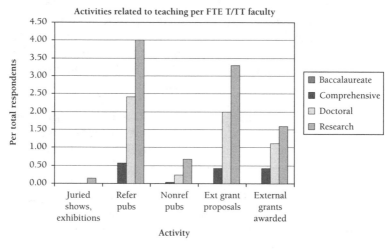

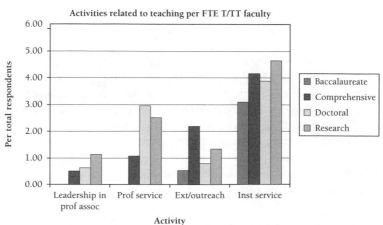

curriculum. It is no surprise that there is an upward trend from baccalaureate to research institutions for activities related to scholarship such as referred and nonrefereed publications, as well as external grant proposals and external grants awarded. All institutions, regardless of Carnegie classification, focus on extension and outreach and institutional service. It is worthy to note that a typical tenured or tenure track faculty member engages in an average of three to five distinct activities related to institutional service per year. These activities might relate to faculty governance, faculty committees, peer mentoring, academic programs in residences, recruiting efforts, student activity advisor, or other student activity involvement.

The Out-of-Classroom Faculty Activity Study has three primary uses. First, the study offers some measure of quantification of out-of-classroom faculty activity as a context for examining the standard teaching load and instructional cost benchmarks generated annually by the Delaware Study. Second, the type of activities reported by faculty should help underscore institutional missions. For example, faculty at research and doctoral institutions might be expected to engage in traditional measures of scholarship—publishing, research, and public service—while faculty at comprehensive and baccalaureate institutions might be involved more with activity directly engaging students—academic advising, supervision of interns, and undergraduate research. Third, the data collected should help to underscore the types of scholarship and other activities in which faculty engage across the disciplines. For example, fine arts and performing arts faculty do not publish; they perform. In addition, the volume of sponsored research and service activity in the sciences, engineering, and agricultural sciences might be expected to be significantly larger than in the humanities.

The Out-of-Classroom Faculty Activity Study helps articulate the difference between what faculty are *expected* to do outside of the classroom, on the basis of institutional mission, and what faculty *actually* do outside the classroom. Essentially the Out-of-Classroom Faculty Activity Study can be used as a management tool for assessing the extent to which an institution is fulfilling its mission. The study should help alleviate misunderstandings by furnishing information to discuss what faculty actually do, how much they do, and the associated products.

Conclusions and Summary

An Office of Institutional Research must clearly communicate the complete picture of faculty activity to individuals within and external to higher education. What faculty do, how much they do, how well they do it, and the associated costs need to be transparent. The only way to accomplish this is to offer a means for this type of information to be collected, ensure accuracy, and encourage utility. Once the Office of Institutional Research understands the complete picture of faculty work at a given institution, it will play a key role in describing such work.

References

Cataldi, E. F., Bradburn, E. M., Fahimi, M., and Zimbler, L. *2004 National Study of Postsecondary Faculty (NSOPF:04): Background Characteristics, Work Activities, and Compensation of Instructional Faculty and Staff: Fall 2003* (NCES Publication No. NCES 2006-176). U.S. Department of Education. Washington, D.C.: National Center for Education Statistics, 2005. Retrieved Dec. 21, 2005, from National Center for Education Statistics (http://nces.ed.gov/pubsearch/pubsinfo.asp?pubid=2006176).

Center for Postsecondary Research. *Faculty Survey of Student Engagement (FSSE)*, 2008. Retrieved Jan. 9, 2008, from http://fsse.iub.edu/index.cfm.

DeGeorge, R. T. *Academic Freedom and Tenure: Ethical Issues.* Lanham, Md.: Rowman and Littlefield, 1997.

Higher Education Research Institute (HERI). *The HERI Faculty Survey*, 2007. Retrieved Dec. 31, 2007, from http://www.gseis.ucla.edu/heri/facoverview.php.

Middaugh, M. F. (2001). *Understanding Faculty Productivity: Standards and Benchmarks for Colleges and Universities.* San Francisco: Jossey-Bass.

Middaugh, M. F., Graham, R., and Shahid, A. *A Study of Higher Education Instructional Expenditures: The Delaware Study of Instructional Costs and Productivity (NCES 2003-161).* Washington, D.C.: U.S. Department of Education, 2003.

National Center for Education Statistics (NCES). *National Study of Postsecondary Faculty (NSOPF*; n.d.). Retrieved Dec. 31, 2007, from http://nces.ed.gov/surveys/nsopf/.

MICHAEL F. MIDDAUGH *is assistant vice president for institutional research and planning at the University of Delaware, as well as past president of both the Association for Institutional Research and the Society for College and University Planning, a commissioner and vice chair of the Middle States Commission on Higher Education, and the national director of the Delaware Study of Instructional Costs and Productivity.*

HEATHER A. KELLY *is the assistant director of institutional research and planning at the University of Delaware and the associate director of the Delaware Study of Instructional Costs and Productivity.*

ALLISON M. WALTERS *is an institutional research analyst at the University of Delaware and is data manager for the Delaware Study of Instructional Costs and Productivity.*

5

Institutional researchers can provide valuable information about student populations. Which of the myriad institution-specific research studies that are currently conducted are most valuable?

Typical Institutional Research Studies on Students: Perspective and Examples

Anne Marie Delaney

Institutional research can enhance an institution's competitive advantage through admission research by comparing the characteristics of inquirers who apply with those who do not; by documenting trends in the characteristics of applicants; and by conducting studies of accepted students, comparing those who matriculate with those who do not. Retention studies are an opportunity to link admission criteria to student performance in college. Studies on current students offer a basis for evaluating the academic program and student life. Finally, alumni studies present a unique chance to elicit graduates' evaluation of their education from the perspective of their postgraduate life and work experience.

Enhancing the Institution's Competitive Advantage Through Admission Research

Literature on admission research constitutes a theoretical and empirically based foundation to guide researchers who are designing admission studies. In an early work, Hossler and Gallagher (1987) proposed a three-stage model of college choice: the first or predisposition stage is one in which familial, societal, and economic factors generate interest and attitudes conducive to college enrollment; the search stage occurs when college-bound students proactively explore potential institutional options or choice sets and evaluate their academic and financial capabilities in relation to these potential choices; and the third and final stage is one in which students make their selection from available options. Hossler, Braxton, and Coopersmith (1989) explain why research is important at each stage of the

NEW DIRECTIONS FOR HIGHER EDUCATION, no. 141, Spring 2008 © Wiley Periodicals, Inc.
Published online in Wiley InterScience (www.interscience.wiley.com) • DOI: 10.1002/he.293

college choice process. In the predisposition stage, it documents the importance of parental involvement and the fact that most students make their postsecondary plans by the end of the ninth or tenth grade. Research at the search stage indicates that the role of admission test taking and academic tracking must be taken into account. Research at the final stage can enable administrators to improve marketing activities and selection of students who best fit the institution.

An extensive number of empirical studies have documented the influence of student and institutional characteristics on college choice. Student characteristics include family income (Flint, 1992) and students' ability (Galotti and Mark, 1994). Institutional characteristics involve the quality of staff and faculty, types of degree programs, faculty-student interaction, and financial assistance (Coccari and Javalgi, 1995); and good academic reputation, affordability, good job placement, and well-managed facilities (Comm and LaBay, 1996). Kallio (1995) reports that graduate student decisions are affected by some of the same factors influencing undergraduate students, but they differ with a greater influence of spouse, family, and work issues. The following sections describe typical admission studies that focus primarily on the search and choice stages. The discussion highlights methodological issues, topics, and policy implications of these studies.

Inquiry Studies. Administrators aspiring to increase the pool of applicants to their institution may obtain valuable information from an inquiry study. The population should include those who inquired about the institution during a specific period of time, with analyses comparing the responses of those who subsequently applied and those who did not apply. Relevant topics include respondents' number of inquiries and applications, identification of top competitor institutions, ratings on the helpfulness of information resources, evaluation of the timeliness and adequacy of the institution's response to the inquiry, and reasons for not applying to the institution. Information on respondent characteristics, including gender, age, citizenship, racial or ethnic background, and academic qualification, should also be obtained.

Applicant Studies. The number of applications has implications for institutional revenue and student selectivity. Institutional research can serve a vital function in monitoring trends in applications and applicant characteristics. Applicant trend studies yield crucial information to achieve the institution's enrollment goals. Documented trends in applicants' demographic, personal, and academic characteristics are a basis for developing effective recruitment strategies to increase the geographic and ethnic diversity of the student population, balance the male-female ratio, and improve the academic quality of the student population.

Accepted Student Studies. Surveys of accepted students amount to a vehicle for enhancing understanding of students' enrollment decision process and for identifying top competitor schools. These studies typically address a number of questions: Which institutional characteristics are important to students' choice? How do students rate the institution and top competitors on these characteristics? Which institutions are the top competitor schools? How do students evaluate their admission experience? What role does financial aid play in students' enrollment decision?

Results from admitted student surveys can be a basis for comparing the enrollment decision processes of matriculants and nonmatriculants and of particular subgroups, such as women, academically talented students, international students, and racial and ethnic minorities. Administrators can use results from accepted student surveys to identify areas for improvement in the admission process, design recruitment strategies to attract particular subpopulations, develop financial aid policies, and identify program and institutional characteristics that need to be strengthened to increase the yield with the institution's accepted student population.

Monitoring Student Progress: Linking Admission Criteria to Student Performance

Retention research in higher education is extensive and dates back to the 1970s (Reason, 2003). Both the theoretical and the empirical retention literature are useful in designing studies and identifying the data elements required for retention research. In *Preventing Students from Dropping Out*, Astin (1975) identified student characteristics—such as high school grade, admission test scores, gender and race, and institutional characteristics (including type, location, and selectivity) that affect retention. In *Leaving College: Rethinking the Causes and Cures of Student Attrition*, Tinto (1987) presents a conceptual theory that explains retention in terms of social and academic integration into the institution. Tinto's theory guided much of the retention research in the 1990s. Peltier, Laden, and Matranga (1999) identified these predictors of retention: gender, race and ethnicity, socioeconomic status, high school grade point average, and college grade point average. Reason (2003) proposes that the increasing diversity of college students requires reevaluation of those variables previously understood to predict retention.

There are two types of retention study: a short-term analysis or snapshot that documents the number and percentage of students in each class returning each semester and a longitudinal retention study of a particular student cohort, that is, an entering freshman class. A longitudinal study supplies a means of linking admission criteria to student performance, and it offers more in-depth information regarding the relationship of student characteristics and college experiences to retention. The institution's administrative data is the primary database for a longitudinal retention study. The potential for research is significantly enhanced if administrative data can be merged with student survey data, such as the Cooperative Institutional

Research Program (CIRP) entering freshman survey, the Your First College Year (YFCY)[1] survey, and the graduating senior survey. Merging these data files is relatively simple if a common ID is used.

Astin (1993) proposes creation of a longitudinal retention file as the best long-term solution for assessment; he offers the Input—Environment—Output (I-E-O) model for this type of study. The model is based on the assumption that one needs information about the characteristics of incoming students (inputs) in order to evaluate the impact of educational programs and experiences (environment) on outcomes. Illustrative inputs include demographic variables (gender and citizenship) and admission characteristics (SAT scores and admission ratings). Self-reported academic and social college experiences represent the environment. Graduation status, grade point averages, and student satisfaction are examples of outcomes.

Evaluating Enrolled Students' Experience: Assessing Student Success and Satisfaction

Through a systematic survey research program, institutional researchers can enhance understanding of students from entrance to postgraduation. Two types of student survey may be used: standardized and custom-designed. A customized instrument can focus attention on priority institutional issues. Standardized surveys are professionally designed to meet measurement criteria and provide national norms for comparison. A third option of using a customized instrument with some items common to a national survey offers the advantage of addressing priority institutional concerns and having national norms. This section presents examples of research based on each of these options.

Entering Freshmen. The Cooperative Institutional Research Program Survey (CIRP) is a national longitudinal survey of first-time, full-time freshmen in the United States, which has been administered for forty-one years. Entering freshman respondents furnish information on a range of topics, notably reasons for attending college, reasons for choosing this college, self-ratings of their abilities, goals, values and expectations of the college experience, career plans, and aspirations for the future. CIRP survey reports include institution specific profiles summarized by gender, with comparative national norms for institutions of similar types. Researchers can also access the data for further analyses. This is an opportunity to conduct more in-depth analyses on issues of particular concern to the institution.

First-Year Experience. Barefoot (2000) observed that the global emergence of first-year programs over the last two decades reflects the higher education community's realization of the significance of the freshman year. Results from empirical studies document the significant impact of first-year college experiences on a range of student outcomes, among them academic success, intellectual growth, retention, and satisfaction. Gerken and Volkwein (2000) found that the strongest predictors of eleven of twelve college

NEW DIRECTIONS FOR HIGHER EDUCATION • DOI: 10.1002/he

outcomes were the vitality of student interaction with faculty and with each other during the freshman year. However, further research is needed to ensure that first-year-experience programs realize the potential for success. Upcraft, Gardner, and Barefoot (2005) noted that although the last two decades have witnessed increased efforts to improve the first year of college, many challenges remain—in particular, a low first-year academic success rate, a first-year experience less academically challenging than students expect, and inadequate attention to enhancing student learning in the first year.

Your First College Year (YFCY) survey is designed for research on the first-year experience. The survey is administered at the end of the first year and addresses several aspects of students' experience: perceived growth; level of academic adjustment; and satisfaction with the academic program, student services, and overall college experience. Also, individual responses from the YFCY are linked to CIRP survey responses obtained at the beginning of the first year. This merged data amounts to a basis for assessing changes in student characteristics, values, and goals during the first year. A brief description of studies based on YFCY data follows.

In *The First Year in College: Understanding What Makes a Difference,* Delaney (2004a) addressed the question, "What student characteristics and freshman year experiences significantly predict students' overall satisfaction with the first year?" Regression results identified satisfaction with sense of community, success in developing close friendships, satisfaction with campus resources and the quality and relevance of courses, and participation in student clubs as statistically significant predictors of overall satisfaction. These variables explained 53 percent of the variance in students' overall satisfaction with the first year.

In another study on the first-year experience, Delaney (2007b) examined the impact of faculty-student interaction on student outcomes. The study identified significant relationships between interaction with faculty and perceived growth in knowledge, academic adjustment, and satisfaction with courses. Regression analysis revealed that, after controlling for relevant factors, interaction with faculty significantly predicted academic performance, and satisfaction with faculty contact significantly predicted overall satisfaction.

A third study focused on students' social and cultural values (Delaney, 2007a). Results revealed that students who were committed to improving their understanding of other cultures; who held strong social, cultural values; and who perceived growth in knowledge of other races and cultures were more likely to socialize with someone of another race or culture in the first year.

Graduating Seniors' Assessment

A survey of graduating seniors is an ideal vehicle for eliciting students' evaluation of their college experience. Two major topics typically addressed in a senior survey are students' perception of growth in knowledge and ability and their satisfaction with programs and services. Senior survey research may be based on a custom-designed survey, a national survey, or a custom-designed instrument that includes items common to a national survey. Examples of national surveys are the Higher Education Data Sharing (HEDS) Consortium Senior Survey; the College Senior Survey (CSS), sponsored by the HERI at UCLA; and the National Survey of Student Engagement (NSSE), sponsored by the Indiana University Center for Postsecondary Research.

Nelson and Johnson (1997) identified how senior surveys could serve as a vehicle for achieving program improvement in the curriculum, career services, and student advising. Cheng's research (2001) is an excellent example of how an externally developed senior survey may be used to construct a model for assessing the student collegiate experience and producing outcome measures in an institution's assessment effort.

Delaney (2005) presents a model for designing senior survey research studies to achieve optimum impact on assessment and policy development. Based on trend data for 970 graduating seniors, the paper demonstrates how the link between research and policy was achieved through the conceptual organization, design, and statistical analyses of results. This model involves six steps:

1. Review the institutional mission.
2. Identify the goals of the undergraduate academic program.
3. Define the major components of the undergraduate student life experience.
4. Develop a means to evaluate academic goal achievement and satisfaction with student life.
5. Design a statistical analysis plan to address planning and policy issues.
6. Translate the results into recommendations for planning and policy development.

In *Assessing Undergraduate Education from Graduating Seniors' Perspective: Peer Institutions Provide the Context* Delaney (2001a), demonstrates how a customized survey, with some items common to the HEDS senior survey, was used to compare the satisfaction and evaluation of graduating seniors at the study institution with that of their peers. The study was based on survey responses of 244 graduating seniors from the primary institution and approximately 1,500 students from a diverse group of thirty-nine peer colleges and universities in the United States. On the basis of institutional type and the national ranking schema of *U.S. News and World Report,* the peer institutions were classified in five categories: first-tier colleges; first-tier universities; first- and second-tier colleges; second-, third-, and fourth-tier colleges; and a diverse-tier group. Comparative findings from this study were particularly meaningful because the peers shared the same academic major and were preparing for similar careers in the field of business.

Assessing Program Effectiveness with Alumni Studies

Alumni studies are a means of determining alumni satisfaction with their education. As Hartman and Schmidt (1995) observe, understanding and promoting alumni satisfaction is important given that satisfied alumni are likely to help the college financially, offer positive word-of-mouth communication, and offer jobs to subsequent graduates. Pearson (1999) determined that alumni who were very satisfied also perceived the value of their college education to be greater, took pride in their degree, had a stronger personal commitment to the institution, and were more likely to be donors. Martin and others (2000) discovered that alumni who were more satisfied with their institution thought they were better prepared for employment.

For some time, researchers have emphasized the crucial role of alumni in assessment of higher education's effectiveness. Williford and Moden (1989) noted that alumni offer a unique contribution in assessing the quality of their education tempered by their experiences since graduation. Khalil (1990) claimed that alumni potentially offer an objective perspective given their distance from involvement with the program. Lee Harvey (2000) recommends using perceptual studies of alumni to assess how well higher education is preparing graduates with the appropriate personal and intellectual skills needed in the workplace.

One major consideration in designing an alumni study is whether the primary focus should be on evaluating the educational program or on monitoring graduates' personal and professional development. Recent classes should be selected if the primary purpose is to evaluate the curriculum; earlier classes should be selected if the primary purpose is to study graduates' career paths and postgraduate personal and professional development.

In the article "Ideas to Enhance Higher Education's Impact on Graduates' Lives: Alumni Recommendations," Delaney (2004b) presents a model for research with a primary focus on evaluating the curriculum. The study was based on a survey of about five hundred undergraduate alumni from a private college in the northeastern United States. Two major areas addressed were satisfaction and perceived growth attributed to the college experience. Consistent with the principles of good practice in assessment, the survey for this study was designed to reflect the goals of the undergraduate curriculum (Banta, Lund, Black, and Oblander, 1996). Results identified these significant predictors of overall satisfaction: satisfaction with a sense of community; satisfaction with preparation for one's future career; and perception of enhanced abilities to acquire new knowledge, communicate well orally, and understand others. These findings indicate that graduates evaluate their education through the prism of several aspects of their experience: the quality of community life during college, the adequacy of career preparation, and enhanced capacity for lifelong learning and relating with others.

Discovering Success Strategies Through Alumnae/i Research (Delaney, 2002) presents a research model focused primarily on studying the career paths and professional development of alumni. The model was designed from a review of theoretical and empirical literature on career development. Results from more than three hundred business major alumni identified a number of correlates of career success: high-risk orientation, high-achievement motivation, and a positive attitude toward globalization and opportunities to acquire broad management experience, negotiate business deals, and achieve success on a critical project. Based on these findings, the final report recommended that the college should design programs to develop attitudes correlated with success and encourage students to seek the types of career opportunities found to enhance success. Thus the study demonstrates how alumni research may be used to enhance higher education's effectiveness in preparing students for success in their career.

Methodological Approaches and Data Sources for Institutional Research on Students

Quantitative and qualitative research approaches are essential to produce the necessary information to support institutional planning for student programs and services. Quantitative methods, traditionally used in institutional research, furnish valuable information about outcomes. Results are useful in summative decision making. However, qualitative methods are necessary to explain the *why* of results and to support formative decision making for improvement (Howard and Borland, 2007).

Primary and secondary data sources are available for research on students. Surveys and focus groups are examples of primary data sources; using both presents an opportunity to produce outcome data and explain the reasons for the outcomes. Examples of secondary data sources are the institution's administrative database, consortia datasets, and national datasets available from the National Education Data Resource Center.

Requirements for Successful Institutional Research on Students

To realize the goal of enhancing administrators' understanding of students through research, higher education administrators and institutional researchers need to have a shared perspective regarding the role of institutional research. As several authors have noted, administrators' perception of the role of institutional research is crucial: "When institutional research is perceived simply as a number-crunching activity, not only does the profession lose, but so does each and every institution where this attitude prevails" (Presley, 1990, p. 106). Echoing a similar theme, Olsen (2000) observed that although the practice of institutional research involves production of data, the art is contextualizing the data and converting it into meaningful information. Terenzini (1993) describes contextual intelligence as the highest form of intelligence that earns institutional researchers legitimacy, trust, and respect.

NEW DIRECTIONS FOR HIGHER EDUCATION • DOI: 10.1002/he

Administrators' Role. Administrators play a critical role in enabling institutional researchers to produce successful studies. Effective administrators articulate policy relevant questions, value research, facilitate access to resources, and use the results of research in decision making. Ehrenberg (2005), a former vice president who supervised the Office of Institutional Research at Cornell University, emphasizes the need to educate administrators about the usefulness of institutional research, particularly if they are not data-driven.

Researcher Qualifications. Several studies highlight the importance of researcher qualifications and level of education to institutional researchers' effectiveness. Volkwein (1999) observed that the role of the institutional researcher as policy analyst requires a relatively high level of education and training as well as both analytical and issues intelligence. Terenzini (1999) noted that acquiring the methodological and analytical skills relevant to institutional research is most likely to be sound and complete when received in formal coursework in such areas as research design, measurement, sampling, statistics, and qualitative research methods. Delaney (2001b) found that institutional researchers with a doctorate reported significantly more often that their work had resulted in program or policy changes at their institution.

Characteristics of Effective Institutional Research Studies. To be effective in influencing planning and policy, institutional research studies must be based on sound methodology. They should focus on policy relevant questions and be action-oriented for decision making. Research reports should present information based on analysis of the data. Finally, to achieve optimum influence on policy, research reports should include recommendations formulated on the basis of results. Research has shown that assuming a proactive role by formulating recommendations and conducting follow-up studies enhances the potential for influencing policy (Delaney, 2001b).

Note

1. The first two surveys of the three are produced by the Higher Education Research Institute (HERI) at the University of California, Los Angeles.

References

Astin, A. W. *Preventing Students from Dropping Out*. San Francisco: Jossey-Bass, 1975.

Astin, A. *Assessment for Excellence*. Phoenix: American Council on Education and the Oryx Press, 1993.

Banta, T. W., Lund, J. P., Black, K. E., and Oblander, F. W. *Assessment in Practice*. San Francisco: Jossey-Bass, 1996.

Barefoot, B. "The First-Year Experience—We Making It Any Better?" *About Campus*, 2000, 4(6), 12–18.

Cheng, D. X. "Assessing Student Collegiate Experience: Where Do We Begin?" *Assessment & Evaluation in Higher Education*, 2001, 26(6), 525–538.

Coccari, R. L., and Javalgi, R. G. "Analysis of Students' Needs in Selecting a College or University in a Changing Environment." *Journal of Marketing for Higher Education,* 1995, *6*(2), 27–39.

Comm, C. L., and LaBay, D. G. "Repositioning Colleges Using Changing Student Quality Perceptions: An Exploratory Analysis." *Journal of Marketing for Higher Education,* 1996, *7*(4), 21–34.

Delaney, A. M. "Assessing Undergraduate Education from Graduating Seniors' Perspective: Peer Institutions Provide the Context." *Tertiary Education and Management,* 2001a, *7*(3), 255–276.

Delaney, A. M. "Institutional Researchers' Perceptions of Effectiveness." *Research in Higher Education,* 2001b, *42*(2), 197–210.

Delaney, A. M. "Discovering Success Strategies Through Alumnae/i Research." Paper presented at the 42nd annual forum of the Association for Institutional Research, Toronto, Canada, June 2002.

Delaney, A. M. "The First Year in College: Understanding What Makes a Difference." Paper presented at the 26th annual forum of the European Association for Institutional Research, Barcelona, Spain, Sept. 2004a.

Delaney, A. M. "Ideas to Enhance Higher Education's Impact on Graduates' Lives: Alumni Recommendations." *Tertiary Education and Management,* 2004b, *10*(1), 89–105.

Delaney, A. M. *Expanding Students' Voice in Assessment Through Senior Survey Research* (Professional File, No. 96). Tallahassee, Fla.: Association for Institutional Research, Summer 2005.

Delaney, A. M., "Do International and U.S. College Freshmen Share Social and Cultural Values?: Implications for Integration." Paper presented at the 47th annual forum of the Association for Institutional Research, Kansas City, Mo., June 2007a.

Delaney, A. M. "Why Faculty-Student Interaction Matters in the First Year Experience." Paper presented at the 29th annual forum of the European Association for Institutional Research, Innsbruck, Austria, Aug. 2007b.

Ehrenberg, R. G. "Why Universities Need Institutional Researchers and Institutional Researchers Need Faculty Members More Than Both Realize." *Research in Higher Education,* 2005, *46*(3), 349–363.

Flint, T. A. "Parental and Planning Influences on the Formation of Student College Choice Sets." *Research in Higher Education,* 1992, *33*(6), 689–708.

Galotti, K. M., and Mark, M. C. "How Do High School Students Structure an Important Life Decision? A Short-Term Longitudinal Study of the College Decision-Making Process." *Research in Higher Education,* 1994, *35*(5), 589–607.

Gerken, J. T., and Volkwein, J. F. "Precollege Characteristics and Freshman Year Experiences as Predictors of 8-year College Outcomes." Paper presented at the annual forum of the Association for Institutional Research, Cincinnati, Ohio, May 2000.

Hartman, D. E., and Schmidt, S. L. "Understanding Student/Alumni Satisfaction from a Consumer's Perspective: The Effects of Institutional Performance and Program Outcomes." *Research in Higher Education,* 1995, *36*(2), 197–217.

Harvey, L. "New Realities: The Relationship Between Higher Education and Employment." *Tertiary Education and Management,* 2000, *6*(1), 3–17.

Hossler, D., and Gallagher, K. S. "Studying Student College Choice: A Three-Phase Model and the Implications for Policymakers." *College and University,* 1987, *62*(3), 207–221.

Hossler, D., Braxton, J., and Coopersmith, G. "Understanding Student College Choice." In J. C. Smart (ed.), *Higher Education Handbook of Theory and Research, Vol. 5.* New York: Agathon Press, 1989.

Howard, R. D., and Borland, K. W. "The Role of Mixed Method Approaches in Institutional Research." In R. D. Howard (ed.), *Using Mixed Methods in Institutional Research.* Tallahassee, Fla.: Association for Institutional Research, 2007.

Kallio, R. E. "Factors Influencing the College Choice Decisions of Graduate Students." *Research in Higher Education,* 1995, *36*(1), 109–124.

Khalil, E. M. (ed.). *Academic Review of Graduate Programs: A Policy Statement.* Washington, D.C.: Council of Graduate Schools, 1990. (ERIC Document Reproduction Service no. ED 331 421).

Martin, A. J., and others. "Graduate Satisfaction with University and Perceived Employment Preparation." *Journal of Education and Work,* 2000, *13*(2), 199–213.

Nelson, E. S., and Johnson, K. A. "A Senior Exit Survey and Its Implications for Advising and Related Services." *Teaching of Psychology,* 1997, *24*(2), 101–105.

Olsen, D. "Institutional Research." In L. K. Johnsrud and V. J. Rosser (eds.), *The Work and Career Paths of Midlevel Administrators.* New Directions for Higher Education, no. 111. San Francisco: Jossey-Bass, 2000.

Pearson, J. "Comprehensive Research on Alumni Relationships: Four Years of Market Research at Stanford University." In J. Pettit and L. H. Litten (eds.), *A New Era of Alumni Research.* New Directions for Institutional Research, 1999, *26*(1) 5–21.

Peltier, G. L., Laden, R., and Matranga, M. "Student Persistence in College: A Review of Research." *Journal of College Student Retention,* 1999, *1*(4), 357–375.

Presley, J. B. "Putting the Building Blocks into Place for Effective Institutional Research." In P. T. Terenzini and E. E. Chaffee (series eds.) and J. B. Presley (vol. ed.), *Organizing Effective Institutional Research Offices.* New Directions for Institutional Research, no. 66. San Francisco: Jossey-Bass, 1990.

Reason, R. D. "Student Variables That Predict Retention: Recent Research and New Developments." *NASPA Journal,* 2003, *40*(4), 172–191.

Terenzini, P. T. "On the Nature of Institutional Research and the Knowledge and Skills It Requires." *Research in Higher Education,* 1993, *34*(1), 1–10.

Terenzini, P. T. "On the Nature of Institutional Research and the Knowledge and Skills It Requires." In *What Is Institutional Research All About? A Critical and Comprehensive Assessment of the Profession.* New Directions for Institutional Research, no. 104. San Francisco: Jossey-Bass, 1999.

Tinto, V. *Leaving College: Rethinking the Causes and Cures of Student Attrition.* Chicago: University of Chicago Press, 1987.

Upcraft, M. L., Gardner, J. N., and Barefoot, B. O. (eds.). *Challenging and Supporting the First-Year Student.* San Francisco: Jossey-Bass, 2005.

Volkwein, J. F. "The Four Faces of Institutional Research." In J. F. Volkwein (ed.), *What Is Institutional Research All About? A Critical and Comprehensive Assessment of the Profession.* New Directions for Institutional Research, no. 104. San Francisco: Jossey-Bass, 1999.

Williford, A. M., and Moden, G. O. "Using Alumni Outcomes Research in Academic Planning." Paper presented at the annual forum of the Association for Institutional Research, Baltimore, May 1989.

ANNE MARIE DELANEY *is director of institutional research at Babson College in Wellesley, Massachusetts.*

6

Institutions are increasingly called on to supply evidence that their educational mission is being achieved. The accreditation self-study is one opportunity to exploit the expertise of the institutional research office in collecting important data for institutional improvement.

Accreditation and Institutional Research: The Traditional Role and New Dimensions

Barbara Brittingham, Patricia M. O'Brien, Julie L. Alig

American regional accreditation[1] serves two basic functions: quality assurance and quality improvement. Through its public function of quality assurance, accreditation signals to prospective students, parents, employers, and others that the institution meets fundamental standards of quality. Through its private function of quality improvement, accreditation supplies institutions with a useful engine to foster improvement. In this chapter, we discuss the traditional role of institutional research in an institution's preparation for accreditation—a role most aligned with the quality assurance function of accreditation—and suggest two new dimensions to strengthen the role of the institutional research office that are more aligned with the quality improvement function of accreditation. For the traditional role and new dimensions, we suggest specific action steps for the institutional researcher.

We write from a basic premise: the self-study for accreditation offers opportunities for the institutional research office to advance its basic function and for presidents and provosts to increase the ability of the institution to use and rely on evidence and data for institutional improvement. Here are the suggestions.

Traditional Role for Institutional Research: Involvement and Support

Serve on the Self-Study Steering Committee. When the time comes for a comprehensive evaluation, many institutions appoint the institutional

NEW DIRECTIONS FOR HIGHER EDUCATION, no. 141, Spring 2008 © Wiley Periodicals, Inc.
Published online in Wiley InterScience (www.interscience.wiley.com) • DOI: 10.1002/he.294

researcher to the self-study team—a practice we highly endorse. The institutional researcher can be a valuable resource to the team in ways we outline here. Speaking to the chief academic officer in advance of the self-study process can help increase the probability of an appointment because eager volunteers are a valuable asset.

Thus, even though appointment to work on a committee writing a specific standard is possible, an institutional researcher might more helpfully and more powerfully serve as a resource for all writing committees as, for example, they consider judicious use of tables, graphs, and other data displays to supplement the narrative of the self-study. The institutional researcher understands that data are meant to "tell a story" about the institution and can assist the self-study's writers in deciding which data are the most effective means through which to tell a particular story and how the data can be most effectively displayed.

Take Responsibility for Getting the Data Forms Completed. All accreditors ask their member institutions to submit data in standardized formats so that their trained volunteers, who are members of teams and commissions, can count on having consistently defined and presented information from every institution going through the process. Some of the required information can be supplied directly from the IR office itself with data that are part of its bread-and-butter work (enrollment data, for example) while other information requires the assistance of other specialized offices (such as the financial aid office).

Self-study teams often wait until the narrative part of the self-study is completed before turning to completing the data forms. Institutional research offices can support a better process by ensuring that the forms are filled out early in the process. Doing so gives the institutional research office sufficient time to assemble all the data and ensure their accuracy but, perhaps more important, enables the members of the self-study team to use the information represented in the forms and ensure that the numbers and the text tell the same story about the institution.

For institutions with multiple accreditors, establishing the institutional researcher as a contact person with the various associations can facilitate conversation between the institution and the accreditors about the data that are needed and the exact form in which they are reported. If, for example, the institution is already collecting and reporting data in a form similar to that requested by the accreditor, it may be possible to suggest substituting those data for the particular information or format requested by the accreditor. This conversation is more likely to occur if the institutional researcher is in the position of coordinating all data requests from all accrediting associations, as well as the myriad other data requests submitted to the institution.

Supply the Self-Study Team with Additional, Current, Useful Institutional Data and Reports. Every institution has more data than it uses, and the self-study is an excellent opportunity to develop or improve institutional habits in using information already available. With a solid understanding of data and evidence, the institutional researcher can help the self-study committees think through what would be most helpful to include as evidence. Factbooks, annual reports, survey results, placement studies, exit interviews, and strategic plans are examples of documents that can generate the evidence useful to a self-study committee.

Self-study committee members can identify additional information to support their work. In addition, it may be useful to go beyond what is identified by the committee. Reading the accreditation standards and thinking about what data and evidence the institution already has and what is needed helps institutional researchers identify data they would want as members of a visiting team. Institutional researchers "think data" all of the time, and not all of the members of the self-study team approach the task from this perspective. As the accreditation process becomes more data-driven, getting the data foundation of the self-study report right from the beginning will result in a stronger product and a more favorable presentation of the institution to the visiting team and the accrediting commission.

Identify What Additional Data Are Needed—and Set out to Get It. It often happens that a committee realizes new surveys or research are needed before the self-study can address an issue adequately. For example, the accreditation standards may ask the institution to demonstrate that students use library and electronic resources effectively, increasing their information literacy skills; but the institution may not have yet collected data with this focus. Following this example, the institutional research office has the expertise to work with librarians and faculty members to develop an approach to collect useful information and assist them in understanding the results. Also, rather than have small groups of the self-study team develop their own surveys, it is typically preferable to coordinate this aspect of the data gathering, a coordination that can be attended to by the institutional research office.

Set up an Intranet Site for Exhibits and Catalog What Is Available. At the risk of typecasting institutional researchers, we believe most have the organizational skill to structure presentation of a large number of exhibits so that the team can find what it needs easily and effectively. Many institutional researchers have also established a good working relationship with the institution's information technology staff and are consequently in an excellent position to collaborate on developing an electronic document room, should that be the institution's choice.

Finally, as is true with completion of data forms, concentrating responsibility for organization and presentation of all accreditation exhibits with institutional research ultimately reduces the amount of work involved, as accrediting associations generally require many of the same documents as evidence. Having once determined how best to present these materials, the institutional researcher can reduce the amount of time and effort needed to do it a second time (or a third, or a fourth . . .).

These are the traditional functions for institutional research in a self-study process. Next, we suggest new directions, functions that better support the institution in gaining benefits from accreditation and fostering the type of institutional improvement that is the hallmark of the private function of regional accreditation.

New Dimension One: Developing Capacity to Use Data

Help the Self-Study Team Understand the Data Now Available. Self-study committees typically afford wide representation of the campus community, sometimes including undergraduate students and trustees as well as faculty, administrators, and staff. Almost inevitably there is a range of comfort with data among the self-study team. The institutional researcher can offer support to the team by making sure that the available data are understood sufficiently to be used in the process. For example, though many institutions use surveys of student experiences such as NSSE or CSSE, it is less clear that the results are used systematically by campus groups who can benefit the most from understanding the survey findings. Because members of the self-study committee are likely to vary in their ease in interpreting the data from such surveys, the institutional researcher can play an instructional role with the committee and help them find value in the data. Here the goal goes beyond the self-study process, with the aim of increasing the institution's capacity for and habit in using the data available for improvement.

Help the Institution Define "Success." Regional accreditation relies on the institution's candid assessment of its strengths and weaknesses. The institutional researcher can exercise a vital role in this process by helping campus constituents define success (for a program or the institution as well as the student), select appropriate mechanisms through which to measure those dimensions of success, and develop meaningful forms of presentation so that the measurement results can be easily understood and used to develop plans for improvement. For some institutions, an important component of success is the rate at which students are placed in jobs related to their major within, say, six months of graduation. For other institutions, the rate at which students are admitted to highly regarded law schools or medical schools may be more important. Regional accreditors are open to a variety of ways to look at success, but they are increasingly focused on ensuring that institutions do select, define, measure, and evaluate those dimensions of success important to their mission. The institutional researcher can help with selecting these measures, ensuring they are usefully defined and measured and that results can be tracked systematically over time.

NEW DIRECTIONS FOR HIGHER EDUCATION • DOI: 10.1002/he

Help the Self-Study Committee Understand the Expectations of Accreditors, Translated into Needed Data. Institutional researchers can also help teach self-study committees to translate the standards and requirements into the kinds of evidence needed for the process and useful to the institution. For example, regional accrediting associations ask their members to submit information about all the locations and modalities through which instruction is offered. At a large, complex institution, responsibility for administering offsite locations and distance education programs may be dispersed among a number of offices. Submitting information about all of these activities to a common office can give the institution's senior officers a useful picture of the totality of these initiatives and can facilitate more effective oversight and quality assurance of these endeavors. Such an approach can help the institution think about how it wants to track the retention and graduation rates of off-campus and online students, where traditional IPEDS rates are not useful indicators of success.

Help the Self-Study Committee Learn the Value in "Negative Findings." As we have noted, accreditation is a process of quality assurance that relies on an institution's candid assessment of its strengths and areas for improvement. Such an assessment is not an activity that can be done once a decade, or even once every five years. For an institution to meet its accreditors' expectations regarding ongoing quality improvement, it must develop a culture of inquiry that permeates the campus. Once again, the institutional research office has a critical role to fulfill in developing such a culture.

Establishing a culture of inquiry that says, "We use data here to make decisions" requires support from administrative as well as faculty leadership—and insistence that data be used. This necessitates easy, timely access to reliable, accurate information, which is the purview of the institutional research office. If the institutional research office has a reputation for competence and for reliable data, campus constituents can be confident in their use of data.

The key to establishing a culture of inquiry is willingness to accept "negative results" and use them as the basis for developing realistic plans to address identified weaknesses. This means the campus must be willing to report and use all its assessment results, not just those that present the institution in a good light. In interpreting and using data, the emphasis needs to be on improvement, not on blame. Initial data analysis almost always leads to questions about how the observed results can be explained. The institutional researcher can help ensure that the emphasis is not on explaining away a negative result but rather on determining how the institution needs to change in order to help students be more successful.

Help the Institution Make Progress on Assessment of Student Learning. For the past quarter-century, accreditors have been increasing their focus on institutional effectiveness and student success. Resisting calls

NEW DIRECTIONS FOR HIGHER EDUCATION • DOI: 10.1002/he

for a one-size-fits-all approach to measuring student achievement, accreditors instead have asked institutions to (1) determine definitions of student success appropriate to their mission, (2) adopt meaningful mechanisms through which such success can be measured, and (3) use the results to make improvements to the teaching-and-learning enterprise. In other words, accreditors expect institutions to develop and implement a systematic approach to assessment of institutional effectiveness and student achievement. Truth be told, institutions often set out to make progress in this area faced with the need to do their self-study.

Enter the institutional researcher. And, one hopes, enter the institutional researcher while the assessment plans are being designed rather than after the data are already collected (too often in ways that result in less-than-analyzable results). The institutional researcher may find that the time of the self-study is the teachable moment when it comes to designing or improving an assessment system. Before any data are collected, the institution needs to be clear on what it needs and wants to know and how it will use what it learns. The institutional researcher can be profoundly helpful in shaping such conversations.

With this foundation in place, an institution can think about the data it needs to collect to support its assessment activities. The institutional researcher can help to ensure that the data collected are related to the institution's educational objectives and responsive to the questions that have been asked. The institutional researcher can assist with selecting measures, to ensure an appropriate balance of qualitative and quantitative approaches and of direct and indirect measures of student learning. Because the IR office will store data from year to year, its staff can analyze trends over time and help members of the campus community understand what the trends mean.

Many institutions also choose to compare their performance with that of peer institutions. Once again, the institutional researcher can contribute to these efforts, through assisting in development of a list of peers, establishing a relationship with her or his counterparts at the peer institutions, and presenting the results of the peer analyses such that decision makers on campus can effectively use the data.

New Dimension Two: Evaluation, Planning, and Public Disclosure

Read the Team Report and See How Well the "Evidence Presentation" Worked. With its emphasis on planning and evaluation, much of accreditation is about closing the loop. The institutional researcher can help the institution close the loop for how and how well it presented evidence by reviewing the visiting team's report with a careful eye. How well was the institution's presentation of evidence received by the team? Are there indications that the team found the presentation clear? helpful? distracting? Did the team pick up on key points of success and identified areas for improvement that the institution underscored with evidence? Even though much of the institution's success in this regard depends on the visiting team members, reviewing their report will offer one form of useful feedback.

Read the Action Letter and Begin to Plan for the Next Report. After the self-study and after the team visit, the accrediting commission will make a decision regarding the institution's accreditation; the letter conveying the decision includes information about the date and scope of the next required reports. By reviewing this letter with the institution's academic officer, the institutional researcher can anticipate any further needed studies or analysis and ensure they are prepared well in advance of the deadline. Here it may be useful to meet with key institutional decision makers, reviewing the action letter with them and discussing the data and evidence needed for the next review or report. If data are to be used effectively in making decisions, it is also important for institutional researchers, at least on occasion, to sit around the table with the personnel who are making the decisions. This gives institutional research staff an opportunity to hear what the needs are, help to shape them as necessary, clear up any misunderstandings, and plan effective strategies for meeting the needs of decision makers.

Help to Determine Which Data to Disclose to the Public. Meetings between institutional researchers and decision makers can also be the place to discuss a critical question facing all institutions: What data do we report, and to whom? It is a question that has recently been voiced with greater urgency through increased calls from lawmakers and members of the general public for transparency on the part of institutions. Accreditors' standards include clear expectations about what information an institution must disclose, and increasingly those expectations include data about student success. The institutional researcher can assure them that the factual information disclosed by the institution is accurate and can be a valuable participant in discussions about what other data to disclose, the most effective form in which to present data, and the contextual information that should accompany the information.

A Concluding Comment

In addition to the benefits that accrue to the self-study process from involving the institutional researcher, there is a larger benefit to the institution. Self-studies, particularly those prepared for decennial evaluations by regional accreditors, are an institutional endeavor that involves a range of campus constituents. Involving the institutional researcher in a prominent way in this effort showcases the office and gives faculty, administrators, students, staff, and trustees a clear indication of the value that institutional research can contribute to the institution. It can change how members of the campus community view the institutional research function and increase the likelihood that the institutional researcher will be invited to bring her or his expertise to bear on other major initiatives.

Note

1. We write from the perspective of regional accreditation, but in our observation and experience the principles apply to any institutional accreditation and fit to scale to programmatic or specialized accreditation as well. Also, we concentrate here on the comprehensive evaluation that is carried out in the form of an institutional review every seven to ten years for an institution.

BARBARA BRITTINGHAM is the director of the Commission on Institutions of Higher Education at the New England Association of Schools and Colleges.

PATRICIA M. O'BRIEN is the deputy director of the Commission on Institutions of Higher Education at the New England Association of Schools and Colleges.

JULIE L. ALIG is the assistant director of the Commission on Institutions of Higher Education at the New England Association of Schools and Colleges.

NEW DIRECTIONS FOR HIGHER EDUCATION • DOI: 10.1002/he

7

Data-driven strategic plans yield significant returns for institutions. The author gives an overview of strategic planning and useful techniques that yield meaningful results.

Institutional Research's Role in Strategic Planning

Richard A. Voorhees

Higher education literature is replete with articles and book chapters urging institutions to plan strategically. Escalating demands from higher education boards of trustees and state boards of higher education for institutions to demonstrate their effectiveness are an impetus for institutions to carry out strategic planning. One need not be particularly well informed to have heard calls from Congress, state legislatures, the U.S. Department of Education, and regional and professional accreditation bodies for data-driven evidence to demonstrate that institutions and programs are assessing their outcomes. Still another, and perhaps more compelling, reason for institutions to engage in strategic planning is its promise to help predict and manage the future.

A strategic plan that does not make use of data verges on propaganda. Although customarily appealing in a visual sense, a data-free plan seldom offers a useful framework for gauging an institution's future. In contrast, a strategic plan that focuses on data and uses those data to pose realistic goals and strategies to meet goals portends a significant return for the institution creating it. This pathway is more challenging but infinitely easier to navigate for institutions that have created and maintain an institutional research office.

The Role of Institutional Research

Institutions that have organized and centralized their data enjoy an obvious advantage in grappling with strategic planning and other issues. As the drumbeat for accountability, planning, and demonstrating effectiveness to

internal and external stakeholders intensifies, the stature and importance of institutional research offices on most campuses have grown substantially. The institutional research office is often the first point of contact for faculty and administrators who need data and information to meet internal and external demands. Skillful institutional research personnel enjoy a pivotal role in accessing an institution's data and converting those data into "actionable" information needed for planning.

Developing actionable information intersects with the need that all institutions have to be strategic in their thinking. This chapter seeks to inform campus communities, including faculty and staff, and perhaps also institutional research offices themselves, about the elements of strategic planning that can be combined to create a strategic plan. Together, the techniques that are highlighted here form the basic foundation from which institutions can make rational choices about the future. Most of these techniques emanate from the institutional research office, although they can be executed by other offices or units whose expertise matches the nature of the work.

On many campuses, institutional research exists to generate routine reports required by state, federal, and accreditation agencies. This is a valuable function, especially given the access to institutional data that the institutional research office typically possesses, but if it remains the only function then the institution misses out on significant opportunities. Institutional research offices that spend the majority of their time pursuing excellence in reporting typically have little energy or motivation to look across organizational boundaries to identify new opportunities where their unique skills can benefit the total institution. Examples of extended involvement with the campus can be helpful:

- Basic student outcome research, including retention rate, transfer rate, and graduate employment rate
- More sophisticated student outcome research, including assisting faculty and staff in their efforts to formulate and measure student learning outcomes
- Studies that correlate the institution's curriculum and service offerings with student and employer demands
- Enrollment management research that documents the institution's penetration within key demographic segments
- Focus group research with students and faculty that compare perceptions about the adequacy of institutional services and the teaching-learning equation
- Analysis of competitor institutions located nearby as well as other institutions that compete with the home institution program by program
- Internal program review that informs the institution about why a given program grows, declines, or remains stable

Among these potential projects for institutional research offices can be seen the foundation of a strategic plan. Offices that respond to these challenges are likely to have already pushed themselves beyond a routine reporting function, toward creation of actionable information on behalf of the institution. Such offices are also likely able to assist faculty and staff in understanding actionable information and the complexities raised by seemingly simple questions. Clarifying those questions in ways that can be addressed by an institution's data systems or by new data generated through primary research is a key element in advancing the institution. Not surprisingly, these functions go a long way in creating a nimble institution that responds well to strategic planning.

There exists a persistent myth among many that institutional data are, or should be, "computerized" and therefore instantly available to those who simply know the right keys to press or the correct click of a mouse. In reality, considerable effort must be expended by the institutional research office to gather, clean, edit, and organize data so as to produce correct results. My experience in analyzing these issues for higher education organizations is that unless considerable time and effort have been expended in basic data gathering functions, the amount of work that is purely analytical in nature is proportionally smaller than the "hydraulics" necessary to ensure data quality. Figure 7.1 depicts this relationship.

Elements of Strategic Planning

Stated simply, strategic planning is a process of anticipating change, identifying new opportunities, and executing strategy. Strategic planning can also be described as idea management in which new ideas are developed (or brainstormed), categorized, processed, and implemented. It is a journey that begins best when appropriate data, drawn from multiple sources and using

Figure 7.1.

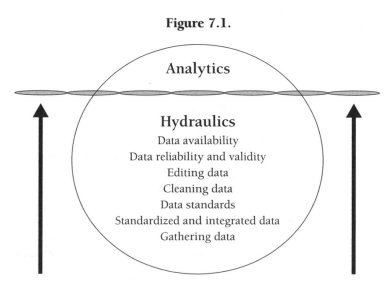

multiple techniques, are transformed into actionable information. Contrasted to "pedestrian information," actionable information makes obvious the next steps an institution should consider. For example, on most campuses understanding that an institution's enrollment is increasing or decreasing is usually conventional wisdom. Understanding which market segments within the overall enrollment are growing and the institution's penetration rate of those segments helps with understanding what actions may be needed to manage growth and should create an appetite for more actionable information.

A successful model for strategic planning incorporates both quantitative and qualitative data collection symbiotically. Tashakkori and Teddlie (2003) suggest three temporal sequences for combining quantitative and qualitative data: (1) concurrently, where two types of data are collected and analyzed in parallel; (2) sequentially, in which one type constitutes a basis for collection of another type; and (3) conversion, where the data are "qualitized" or "quantitized" and analyzed again. Involving faculty and staff in this process is very important if the goal is to ensure that information is valid and translatable to those who will use it. Here we illustrate the blending of qualitative and quantitative techniques in the basic elements of most strategic plans.

In addition to traditional elements commonly found in a strategic plan, I draw on my experiences as a strategic planning facilitator for institutions of higher education to highlight several unique elements that can influence institutional strategy.

Environmental Scan. Virtually every strategic plan features an environmental scan of those external factors and trends that influence an institution's future. An environmental scan requires a volume of information but is helpful only if one knows what within the volume is critical to the development of strategy for that institution. Data for environmental scanning are abundant and grow more so every day on the Internet. Much of these data, however, fall short of criteria for an environmental scan because they lack an actionable connection to the institution. Knowledge of the institution's current operations is required and is most frequently generated by the institutional research office's continuous dialog with key faculty and staff.

Interviewing Key Stakeholders. The need for careful information gathering is illustrated further by skill in interviewing key informants. These interviews can yield helpful qualitative information. A necessary first ingredient is to establish rapport with the interviewee. In general, the more the interviewer prepares for these interviews and the deeper she or he understands basic institutional data, the better the information yielded. Although quantitative data indicate the extent to which outcomes are being met, qualitative interviews speak more to how participants feel about what is happening within an institution. Because mobilizing participants is critical to future actions, deep understanding of their perceptions advances the strategic planning agenda.

NEW DIRECTIONS FOR HIGHER EDUCATION • DOI: 10.1002/he

Focus Groups. The term *focus group* has taken on multiple meanings as a technique such that it is frequently maligned. The term has been used variously to describe casual conversation with more than several people in a random setting—a clear misuse of the concept (Fern, 2001). More appropriately, a focus group is a deliberate event planned to gather specific information. It has a structure that is understood by the facilitator and the participants. Well-planned and executed, focus groups are a qualitative exercise involving a protocol of questions designed to elicit communication while simultaneously not circumscribing meaningful dialog.

Large Group Strategy Sessions. Among the most effective strategic planning techniques in my experience are large group meetings designed to promote an interchange of ideas about strategic issues facing an institution. These sessions are divided between presentation of institutional data, ideally formulated as actionable data, and subsequent discussion by participants. In this way, they differ from focus groups because a strategy session seeks to give everyone a common framework for discussion of institutional strategy.

Properly executed strategy sessions can be an opportunity for key faculty and staff to lend support for the changes that can result from strategic planning. Although the temptation is to label these sessions as focus groups, they are intended to produce two-way learning. In my experience, few stakeholders have been exposed to the concept of actionable data to make meaningful contributions to strategic planning; strategy sessions are a way of educating stakeholders about actionable information and what issues are critical to their institution. Strategy sessions are also a way for the facilitator to learn about what stakeholders see as critical and to capture nuance through deep listening to students, faculty, and administrators and their range of perspectives and opinions.

Geographic Information System (GIS) Maps. Most audiences do not react quickly to presentations of textual or tabular data, especially if the rows and columns are numerous or the font on a PowerPoint presentation obscures easy reading. In these instances, visual information becomes an attractive vehicle for conveying large amounts of data. For example, data drawn from census tracts—small statistical subdivisions of a given county—can illustrate where a given institution should target marketing and recruitment efforts. Geographic information system (GIS) maps offer a quick, visual overview of population changes, including shifts in income, minority subpopulations, age, and housing values, for a strategy session or dissemination across the institution in other ways. Constructing these maps is a quantitative activity, driven by software and technology. Interpreting these maps, on the other hand, is a qualitative activity in which interviewees and strategy session participants offer insight about population shifts that effect the institution.

Competitor Analysis. Few institutions are aware of the range of instructional programs with which they compete for students. The entire institution likely competes for students, but program-by-program competition is increasingly as important to strategy as overall institutional competition. Knowledge generated from this exercise can be the basis for creating new programs or modifying existing ones. It can also point to programs that might be eliminated. Gathering Web information on the programs offered by competitors within proximity to the institution, or from a wider range of institutions that compete regionally or nationally for given instructional programs, is an exercise in tabulating data. The nomenclature needed to describe programs so that they can be categorized accurately is learned best from interviewing academic staff and faculty. Titles of programs may not match their content; astute institutional planners will want to ensure that programs appearing on the surface to compete with their institution's programs are in fact comparable.

Enrollment Forecasting and Scenario Building. Many institutions create enrollment projections, based on a variety of techniques (see, for example, Brinkman and McIntyre, 1997). I have a preference for projecting future institutional enrollments from two key pieces of information: (1) current enrollments at the institution, and (2) actual and projected population counts for the institution's catchment area. Unduplicated headcount data are obtained for the most recently concluded academic year. Population counts and projections are gathered from the U.S. Census Bureau, or ideally from a state or local agency that predicts disaggregated population growth by race, gender, and age. The more disaggregated these data, the more precisely market shares can be established. Second, an increase in precision is also gained if an institution such as a community college or regional state university draws students from a narrow catchment.

Calculating market shares from external data and summing those shares to account for an institution's current enrollment produces a projection that operates in concert with predicted population growth and shifts within those growth patterns. The maximum number of years that an enrollment projection can be expected to be accurate is perhaps no more than twenty. Though a baseline projection is fundamental to strategic planning, it is premised on two assumptions: (1) the institution's current enrollment management techniques, including recruitment and retention activities, will not change during the projection period; and (2) the population projections on which the enrollment projections are based are accurate and remain the same during the projection period. The first assumption does not require the institution to do anything new and for this reason is termed a "status quo" projection.

Use of market segments allows the effect of deliberate institutional decisions to be modeled. These scenarios are developed to demonstrate the effect of increasing a particular segment by a preselected proportion, most often 2 percent over a five-year period. Other, higher thresholds can be set to match the institution's aspirations and capabilities, but 2 percent presents a goal that is widely perceived as within the range of possibility for most institutions. Decision makers are frequently most interested in modeling these scenarios to include increasing shares of minority students, working-age students (most typically, those potential students aged twenty-five to forty-four), and younger students in general.

Instructional Program Vitality. Yet another strategic exercise that cannot be based on numbers alone is analysis of program enrollment data. Upward and downward trends in individual programs are a first place to look when analyzing an institution's instructional menu, but the whole story needs to be researched before conclusions are drawn. For example, it may be that enrollments have declined in response to decisions to limit course availability, combining courses across disciplines, faculty retirements, or lack of program marketing. Each potential reason, and perhaps other considerations, should be balanced against other criteria such as shifts in labor markets, expired curriculum that doesn't match current realities, and actions taken (mostly inadvertently) that discourage enrollment. Without knowledge of these factors, gained qualitatively by listening to stakeholders internal and external to the institution, an incomplete picture of program vitality is more than probable.

Internal and External Surveys. One-on-one interviewing and strategy sessions may not substitute for gathering opinions and insights by way of survey research. Data gathered from existing questionnaires and those developed specifically for planning can furnish multiple perspectives about a college and its environment. A survey can be a traditional paper-and-pencil version or, increasingly, Web-based. Interpreting survey responses is usually regarded as a quantitative activity. Crafting responses that lend themselves to unambiguous interpretation is also a quantitative task; creation of individual survey items, however, draws most often on questions developed during the course of qualitative research.

Analyses of Labor Market Information. The Internet has made labor market information more accessible than ever; it is now easy for colleges to map the connection between the outputs of their career and professional programs and the world of work. Ten-year forecasts are available for new jobs that will be created and for jobs that will grow most rapidly by county, region, state, and nationally. At the national level, these forecasts are connected to the most significant source of postsecondary education or training required for entry in each occupation forecast.

Even though employment forecast data are helpful, strategic planners do not expect a perfect fit between job titles and program labels. The best prediction of academic programs requires knowledge not found in external databases. Insights required to accurately estimate the need for programs match closely those insights necessary to gauge program vitality. Qualitative skill in interviewing techniques (including the aforementioned) entails establishing rapport with interviewees as well as guiding the interview, asking appropriate questions about processes, engaging in empathy for the interviewee, and tabulating interview results. These skills are beyond the scope of this chapter, but they are touchstones for ensuring that qualitative techniques can effectively guide strategic planning.

NEW DIRECTIONS FOR HIGHER EDUCATION • DOI: 10.1002/he

Moving to Operational Planning

A common shortcoming of strategic planning is the failure to connect the dreams and aspirations that arise in strategic planning to specific actions required of operational planning. Many college and university Websites contain visually appealing strategic planning documents, but most do not feature specific actions to support strategy, assignment of responsibility for carrying out those actions, or even more rarely commitment of dollars and human resources to make strategic dreams a reality. There is also a tendency to assign responsibility for action to committees, rather than individuals. Plans of this variety are little more than public relations pieces designed to persuade readers that an institution is carrying out strategy. Mapping the intersection between strategic planning and operational planning requires considerable finesse in blending mixed methodologies.

Action Strategies and Success Factors. As hinted earlier, most strategic plans fall apart because they aren't specific about the actions required to reach goals; nor do they specify a method by which their accomplishment can be measured. To close this gap, faculty and staff should be required to develop specific "action strategies" to support the strategic goals developed during the course of the strategic planning process. This process should be iterative and require both a sense of the possible strategies and success factors that an institution might pursue as well as an estimation of whether they can reasonably be expected to be successful. This is especially the case when the focus is to unite the strategic plan with accountability within the institution for specific results.

Online Planning. Engagement of faculty and staff in strategic planning is related to the transparency of the planning process. To this end, when collecting potential action strategies and success factors across the entire organization an institution should create an online planning Web page. This site can lay out a comprehensive overview of the planning process while seeking new quantitative and qualitative data from all layers of the college to inform—and potentially to collaboratively improve—action strategies and success factors.

Summary and Conclusion

This chapter seeks to give an overview of strategic planning and how institutional research can add value to strategic planning processes for institutions of higher education. It also seeks to enumerate those specific techniques that can be combined to create a meaningful strategic plan. Data and information harvested through these techniques can promote a vision of the institution's future. Certainly, there are other analyses that can be as strategically potent as those suggested here, notably calculating instructional program enrollment trends, matching program outcomes to labor market trends, and understanding one's own institution's instructional productivity.

New Directions for Higher Education • DOI: 10.1002/he

What has been portrayed here are those techniques that institutions should consider as the basic foundation for strategic planning.

References

Brinkman, P., and McIntyre, C. "Methods and Techniques of Enrollment Forecasting." In *Forecasting and Managing Enrollment and Revenue: An Overview of Current Trends, Issues, and Methods.* New Directions for Institutional Research, no. 93. San Francisco: Jossey-Bass, 1997.

Fern, E. F. *Advanced Focus Group Research.* Thousand Oaks, Calif.: Sage, 2001.

Tashakkori, A., and Teddlie, C. (Eds.). *Handbook of Mixed Methods in Social and Behavioral Research.* Thousand Oaks, Calif.: Sage, 2003.

RICHARD A. VOORHEES *is principal of the Voorhees Group LLC, a performance-based consultancy based in Littleton, Colorado.*

NEW DIRECTIONS FOR HIGHER EDUCATION • DOI: 10.1002/he

8

External reporting responsibilities generally fall under the domain of the Institutional Research office, including mandatory data submissions as well as voluntary surveys.

Institutional Research and External Reporting: The Major Data Seekers

Jennifer A. Brown

Institutional research (IR) offices on campus are not all alike, any more than campuses are all alike. They may differ in their reporting line, range of responsibilities, level in the campus hierarchy, and work emphasis. They may differ in some ways by higher education sector—for example, whether the institution is two- or four-year, doctoral or comprehensive, public or private, and whether it is for-profit or not-for-profit. Institutions differ in complexity (number and level of programs, colleges, and schools), size of the student body, affiliation, and other characteristics. All these factors have an impact on the external reporting required of the IR office. The majority of external reports involving IR concern admissions and enrollment data as well as some faculty and staff and finance information. As you will see in this chapter, however, this is not the only area of reporting in which IR may be involved.

External data reporting is focused on higher levels of organizational structure than that necessary for internal reporting. Data are generally collected, for example, about the student characteristics of the total student body, not the student characteristics of those enrolled in each college or school, or each academic department.

Federal reporting guidelines are standard nationally and cover all institutions receiving Title IV funds. States vary in the scope and detail of reporting required by institutions within them. All states require reporting some data from publicly funded institutions. States differ in the extent to which they require regular reporting from private institutions within their boundaries.

NEW DIRECTIONS FOR HIGHER EDUCATION, no. 141, Spring 2008   © Wiley Periodicals, Inc.
Published online in Wiley InterScience (www.interscience.wiley.com) • DOI: 10.1002/he.296

Thus the external reporting responsibilities of IR offices may vary widely depending on the campus.

The information that follows is general and may not exactly match the configuration of responsibilities for an office on any particular campus. However, most IR offices have significant responsibility for external reporting and coordinating of external reports, particularly of admissions and enrollment and degree data.

Mandated Federal Reporting

The Integrated Postsecondary Education Data System (IPEDS), one of the most important of the mandatory reports, is typically the responsibility of the IR office but in some cases the registrar's office. The National Center for Education Statistics, an arm of the U.S. Department of Education, conducts this set of surveys. Although IPEDS has existed since 1987, it was not until 1992 that the federal government mandated compliance. Institutions not in compliance with IPEDS survey completion are easily identified and have been subject to fines.

As higher education policy issues change on the federal level, so do the survey items included in IPEDS. Detailed information on the surveys and the data they contain can be found on the IPEDS Website (http://nces.ed.gov/IPEDS/about/info_collected.asp).

On the campus, it is the responsibility of the president, chancellor, or chief operating officer to designate an IPEDS keyholder for the institution. This is often the individual in charge of IR, to be the campus representative with whom NCES will communicate and who will be responsible for completing or coordinating completion of the annual series of surveys. This individual also needs to keep abreast of changes in IPEDS surveys and prepare the campus data to enable timely compliance.

To comply with federal guidelines, the institution must establish a consistent time in each semester for creating official student and human resources reporting files from which IPEDS data are reported. Specific guidelines also exist for financial reporting timelines. For student reporting, data are drawn from whatever software is used for admissions and registration processing (for example, PeopleSoft or Datatel or a campus-designed system).

The IR office (or computer services under the direction of the IR office) creates and maintains reporting files (often called "frozen," "snapshot," or "census" files), which are saved each semester. Reporting files are drawn from the admissions and registration systems at the same time relative to the start of the semester, every semester. This process ensures that each semester's data are comparable with prior semesters. The exact time selected for the official reporting files varies from campus to campus but is typically after the end of add-drop, when the semester enrollment figures have stabilized and should be within the guidelines established by IPEDS.

NEW DIRECTIONS FOR HIGHER EDUCATION • DOI: 10.1002/he

As the demand for policy data increases and as technology improves, NCES has responded by making submission of the IPEDS survey data electronic and access to the data for purposes of analysis much better. The IPEDS Website is open to the public as well as higher education users. Online query systems enable sophisticated analysis, including peer analysis, to be completed easily.

NCES sends a Data Feedback Report annually to each institution's president and IR office. This contains some of the most frequently requested data on institutional enrollments and finances and compares results for the institution with a set of peers set by NCES or the institution. The Data Feedback Report is not used for any official purpose at present but is sent to demonstrate the usefulness of the IPEDS data to campus leaders.

Your IR office is aware of how the federal definitions or methods for calculation of data in some cases mean that the data differ from the figures used for campus internal analysis. For example, in calculating the percentage of the enrollment in each of the federally mandated categories of race and ethnicity, IPEDS uses total enrollment as the denominator for calculating percentages of students by race or ethnicity. In cases where there are many students who elect not to respond or where there are many "nonresident aliens" (students who are on international visas), the percentage of students of known race will be lower than if the denominator excluded the nonresponses and the nonresident aliens.

In the case of the IPEDS finance survey, the categories of expenditures used in reporting are based on categories developed with the National Association of College and University Business Officers (NACUBO). Although definitions are furnished for which expenditures should be included in which categories (instruction, academic support, and so on), these are open to interpretation and may differ from one institution to another, making peer comparisons of institutional expenditures by type challenging.

IPEDS data are some of the most available and least expensive data on higher education; NCES is working to respond to Congress's requests that such data be made available and useful to consumers of higher education.

One of the tasks of your IR office is to keep up with changes and expansions in data collection and in monitoring public presentation of data to make sure the institution is being represented accurately. IPEDS offers information and training for IR professionals submitting or using IPEDS data in a number of ways, among them online "webinars" in which participants (on their phones and computers in their offices) take a "live" class with other students from around the United States.

As noted earlier, higher education policy issues change over time, and NCES must respond to the changes. A proposal to collect data on each individual student enrolled in higher education was made recently but defeated in Congress after much concern was expressed from the private institutional sector and from privacy advocates. This will most likely lead to a significant expansion of current IPEDS surveys in the next few years.

New Directions for Higher Education • DOI: 10.1002/he

In addition to IPEDS, there are other federally mandated data collected from higher education institutions. For all institutions, the Clery Act requires reporting on campus crime. Information can be found at the U.S. Department of Education Website (http://www.ed.gov/admins/lead/safety/campus.html), which includes campus crime statistics for individual college campuses as well as summary statistics. Your IR office may or may not have responsibility for overseeing reporting of these statistics, which are collected and most often reported by the campus security office. Crimes to be reported under the regulations are alleged (not prosecuted) criminal offenses reported to campus police and are presented under the headings criminal offenses, hate crimes, and arrests.

The National Science Foundation (NSF) also collects data from higher education institutions. Detailed information about the surveys can be found at http://www.nsf.gov/statistics/survey.cfm. The Survey of Earned Doctorates is among the best known of the annual surveys undertaken by NSF, which does survey work in four major areas: education of scientists and engineers, the science and engineering workforce, research and development funding and expenditures, and science and engineering research facilities.

All public institutions of higher education are also mandated to report to the U.S. Bureau of Commerce Census of Government, which takes place every five years. This is a survey of government employment and may be completed by IR or Human Resources depending on the campus organization.

In addition, there are periodic surveys of institutions, which are hard to avoid because they are technically voluntary. These include, for example, the National Postsecondary Student Aid Study (NPSAS), http://nces.ed.gov/surveys/npsas/, which is sponsored by the U.S. Department of Education. The study was first undertaken in 1986-87 and has been repeated every fourth year. The survey requires individual student data from each selected institution and is often coordinated by the IR office, although the president may designate whomever she wishes to do so.

Another example of this type of survey is the recent work of the National Research Council, "An Assessment of Research-Doctorate Programs" (http://www8.nationalacademies.org/cp/projectview.aspx?key=202). The survey developed by the National Research Council required a significant amount of work from the participating IR offices.

Other federal agencies also collect data periodically from universities and colleges. For example, the U.S. Department of Labor Veterans Employment and Training Service collects a survey titled "VETS-100 Federal Contractor Report on Veterans' Employment."

Mandated State and Local Reporting

For most public institutions at all levels and for some private institutions, mandated reporting is also required by the state, which extends financial support for the institution. It is less common for private institutions to be required to report at the state level. For institutions that are part of state systems serving under a single board of trustees or a particular unit of state government, there may be several types of reporting to the various levels of state oversight organizations such as a system board of trustees and department of higher education, or commission of higher education. Other public funding bodies such as counties or cities may also require it.

Most states mandate that IPEDS data be shared with the state higher education agency(s) for their information but also expect reports in more detail than those required by IPEDS or addressing areas of particular policy concern to that state. For example, in Connecticut, state level data by race and ethnicity requires reporting Puerto Rican identity as a category separate from the more general "Hispanic" currently required in IPEDS.

Each state has its own data element definitions, timetable for data submission, and method of data distribution. Definitions of data elements are often similar to those used by IPEDS or the Common Data Set (more on this later), but not necessarily so.

For example, the calculation used to measure the number of full-time-equivalent (FTE) students may differ by state. FTE is a measure used often in planning that makes part-time students "like" full-time students. It is a measure based on the total number of credit hours generated, divided by what is considered to be a full-time credit hour load for undergraduate, master's, or doctoral students. In some states, for example, the denominator might be fifteen for undergraduates, twelve for master's-level credits, and nine for doctoral degree credits. In other states, all graduate credits may be divided by nine. This alters the number of FTE students generated in the calculation.

State-level data collection frequently has two components, data at an aggregate level (for example, the total number of applications, acceptances, and enrollments of new students in a given fall semester) and at a unit record level.

A unit record means a computer record for each student enrolling. This might include demographic characteristics, whether the student is a freshman or transfer, high school GPA, college GPA, SAT scores, high school of graduation, and last college attended. Most states now have at least a modest system of unit record collection in higher education. Efforts by Congress to develop a national higher education unit record system in 2003-04 were not successful, but privately funded efforts are under way. See, for example, the Gates Foundation project "Data Quality Campaign: Using data to Improve Student Achievement" (http://www.dataqualitycampaign.org/), which is working in selected states on unit record systems to track students from prekindergarten through higher education to determine which educational practices and places are most successful in enhancing student success. According to the Education Commission of the States "ECS State Notes," updated in June 2006, "Currently, 30 states are engaged in some kind of P-16 activity" (http://www.ecs.org/clearinghouse/69/26/6926.pdf). In some instances, this means that educational institutions from prekindergarten through four-year college are working together to integrate educational systems and, concomitantly, unit record data systems.

IR offices responsible for student unit record data submission use the frozen files for official reporting as noted above and must often translate the coding and structure of the data to match the requirements of the collecting agency. IR offices at the system or state level then use the data for analysis of statewide trends or individual campus performance.

These systems are becoming increasingly sophisticated with developments in data management and analysis software. In some cases, particularly those in which IR activity is not well developed on campus, the central depository for the data also allows reporting access for the campuses submitting the data. IR offices use these records for campus internal reporting also.

States or systems may require reporting of performance measurement data (which could include financial, human resources, and student data) and of program review data, assessment data, and other reports possibly requiring the coordination or completion by the IR office.

Whether reporting to the academic or administrative leadership of the institution, the IR office is often also involved in supplying data for finance and budget reports for state agencies, trustees, and others in institutional leadership.

Although federal and state reporting is clearly mandatory, there is a process in which institutions participate voluntarily in order to assure themselves that they are maintaining academic quality. This process is accreditation through regional and disciplinary accrediting bodies. The Council for Higher Education Accreditation (http://www.chea.org/default.asp) and the U.S. Department of Education (http://www.ed.gov/admins/finaid/accred/accreditation_pg4.html) include information on accrediting agencies. The existing system of voluntary self-regulation that is the basis for accreditation is a source of debate in higher education, the current secretary of education arguing that the system should be mandatory and under federal control and others that the existing, collegial system is the best way to ensure a reliable and thorough process.

Voluntary or mandatory, the process of accreditation depends on data, much of which is supplied by the campus IR office. IR may also be responsible for helping coordinate the self-study and writing all or part of the self-study report. Whatever the level of IR involvement, the office is critical for a successful accreditation process.

Voluntary Not-for-Profit Reporting

For public institutions, detailed comparative data are available though IPEDS and more detailed state and local data collection. For private institutions seeking peer data, detailed data are not readily available. To fill the gap, there are organizations funded by member institutions that present data sharing opportunities for members. IR offices are often leaders in these efforts. The Higher Education Data Sharing consortium (HEDS) and the Consortium on Financing Higher Education (COFHE) are two examples.

There are also voluntary external data reports in which institutions may elect to participate. One example is the Consortium for Student Retention Data Exchange at the University of Oklahoma (http://www.ou.edu/csrde/). This is a membership organization for those interested in improving their students' success by increasing campus retention and graduation rates. Consortium members supply detailed data, which are then shared without institutional identification.

There are many other examples of voluntary data submission to a variety of organizations, from the National Study of Instructional Costs and Productivity (http://www.udel.edu/IR/cost/) to the Institute of International Education's "Annual Census of International Students" (http://www.iie.org).

Voluntary For-Profit Reporting

As the higher education industry becomes more competitive, the college guide industry has grown—along with concern on the part of institutional researchers about the quantity and quality of the data requested. Discussion of the college guides and their role in informing potential consumers of higher education has been constant during the last decade, with particular focus on the annual *U.S. News and World Report College Guide*. In addition to this publication, institutions are asked to respond to several others, prominently the *College Board, Peterson's, Barron's,* and *Princeton Review.* Institutions do not have to respond to requests for information from these organizations, but typically institution leaders expect that their campus will appear in the publication or on the publication's Website.

The data requested by the college guide publishers continue to grow. For example, the *2008 College Board Annual Survey of Colleges* was fifty pages in length. In an effort to increase the data quality and comparability, several of the college guide publishers work regularly with the Association for Institutional Research and other higher education associations to discuss proposed changes, clarify definitions, and make data available to the data providers. The result of some of this work was development of the Common Data Set or CDS (http://www.commondataset.org/).

IR practitioners often lament that completion of the CDS variables is not sufficient for completion of the college guide surveys. This is because the guides are for-profit enterprises that must, of necessity, distinguish themselves from each other.

Many institutions include the completed CDS on their IR Website, where it can be accessed by the publishers and any other interested readers. For example, the Website of the University of Massachusetts Boston Office of Institutional Research and Policy Studies includes CDS data from 2002 through the most recent submission (http://www.oirp.umb.edu/common_data.html).

NEW DIRECTIONS FOR HIGHER EDUCATION • DOI: 10.1002/he

There have been some voluntary attempts to collect and disseminate CDS data in a manner similar to that used by IPEDS. So far, however, such a system has not been put in place.

In some institutions, the marketing department rather than IR has the final responsibility for submitting data for college guides. Whoever is responsible, the IR office supplies significant amounts of the data.

Princeton Review college guides also use some CDS data, but their data collection method differs significantly from those of the other leading college guides. They conduct "student surveys," sometimes facilitated by campus personnel, and use the results of these surveys to present the comments of students about the institution. Development of a variety of "Best of" designations has enabled the publisher to include an array of institutions. The student survey results used by *Princeton Review* are open to the same methodological concerns as the subjective assessment of college prestige used by *U.S. News and World Report*.

Other sources of information about institutions, such as the New England Board of Higher Education and the Higher Education Directory, typically contain summary statistics institutions have already furnished in IPEDS or the CDS.

Professional Associations

There are additional external reporting responsibilities that do not entirely fit these categories. They are not mandatory, but participation creates useful national data for colleges and universities. The College and University Professional Association or CUPA (http://www.cupahr.org/surveys) and the American Association of University Professors or AAUP (http://www.aaup.org/AAUP) collect data on faculty and faculty salaries. CUPA collects data on faculty salaries by discipline and rank, and data on administrative salaries and employee benefits. AAUP has collected data on faculty salaries for many years and offers analysis of salary trends as well as salaries by higher education sector, and it regularly examines gender equity in faculty salaries.

The National Collegiate Athletic Association or NCAA (http://www.ncaa.org/wps/portal) also requires reporting on student athletes and nonathletes from its members. As Title IX was implemented and concerns rose about the graduation rate of athletes in all divisions, the NCAA focused more on gathering data from institutions. Thus external reporting responsibilities of the IR office may also include NCAA data.

The Future of External Reporting

In the current context of public and legislative concern about higher education accountability, assessment, costs, student learning outcomes, and student success, there is no indication that requests for external reporting will decline in the near future for higher education. New, electronic methods

NEW DIRECTIONS FOR HIGHER EDUCATION • DOI: 10.1002/he

for delivering data to consumers of higher education are proliferating, ranging from the new, free, IPEDS College Navigator tool to the *U.S. News* college rankings interactive Website, which requires payment for access to data and data tools.

Combine this with the proliferation of ever more detailed data presented on individual college and university Websites, and the distinction between internal and external data is becoming more and more permeable. Internal reports are often available to those outside the institution and external survey results are presented to the public by those who collected them.

The recent development of the "Voluntary System of Accountability" under the auspices of the American Association of State Colleges and Universities (http://www.aascu.org/) and the National Association of State Universities and Land-Grant Colleges in a collaborative effort is one example of a voluntary response to the increasing demand for data from colleges and universities.

In this context, it is important to note that external reporting can become so overwhelming for smaller IR offices that it is about all they can manage to accomplish, particularly during the fall semester. When failure to comply with mandatory reporting results in fines or withdrawal of Title IV funding, and when recruitment efforts require completion of college guide surveys, it is difficult for the IR office to put internal data demands at the top of the priority list. Further, as external data requests become more complex and sophisticated, and as they require electronic data submissions—and particularly if they require unit record submission—the technological expertise required of IR professionals grows. Institutional leaders can help by being clear about reporting priorities, and by making sure the IR office staffing meets current reporting needs.

The current movement in higher education to look more closely at the reasons for student success (rather than simply retention and graduation rates) will also add to the kind of work expected of IR offices. Many institutions do not have data systems that easily allow tracking of student enrollment careers from application to graduation (or to leaving the institution). The work envisioned in efforts to understand student success requires more than simply analysis of basic demographic characteristics and number of semesters attended; it requires more detailed examination of patterns of attendance, course taking sequences, and participation in other activities on campus. It also requires use of more data sharing and data exchanges, with such organizations as the National Student Clearinghouse (http://www.studentclearinghouse.org/).

This work is particularly challenging in institutions such as community colleges or urban public four-year institutions, where student attendance and course taking patterns may be very complex. Indeed, studies of "student swirl" show students moving back and forth between institutional types (from two- to four-year and back again) or students who are simultaneously enrolled at more than one institution. These patterns of student attendance are normative for many students, and they challenge more traditional data collection parameters. Add to this mix the proliferation of online education, in which the geographic and temporal locations of the students taking the same course may vary considerably, and the challenges of tracking conditions leading to student success become even more complex and the distinction between internal and external institutional data more blurred.

One of the implications for IR professionals is the need for professional development that keeps pace with changes in technology, data collection, and data collaboration. Another is the need for IR professionals to be fully engaged partners on campus as well as across campuses and other higher education organizations.

JENNIFER A. BROWN is director of Institutional Research and Policy Studies at the University of Massachusetts Boston.

NEW DIRECTIONS FOR HIGHER EDUCATION • DOI: 10.1002/he

REPRISE

Dawn Geronimo Terkla

The intent of this volume is to illustrate for faculty and administrators the work of institutional researchers and how institutional research can provide support and assistance to help further the higher education enterprise.

My initial charge to the authors was to "write a chapter that will describe how institutional research can help faculty and administrators better understand their institutions and the higher education environment." This collection of chapters dispels the myth that IR professionals are simply "bean counters." The authors expound on a variety of areas in which institutional researchers may offer useful insights: assessment, accreditation, strategic planning, faculty workload analysis, peer group identification, benchmarking, comparative institutional analyses, and understanding student populations from prospective applicants to alumni.

In addition to these topics, there are myriad other areas where institutional researchers have or could lend assistance: program evaluation (both academic and administrative), campus climate intelligence, fundraising analysis, curriculum development, formulation of performance and institutional effectiveness measures, and creation of management information tools (such as balanced scorecards and dashboards).

Throughout the pages of this volume, the authors remind us of the importance of institutional researchers' being included in the institutional dialogue. Bringing them into the discussion early allows the institution to be proactive, with the potential of yielding great benefits to the institution. Trudy Bers laments that the most serious barrier affecting IR's ability to contribute to assessing student learning outcomes is that institutional researchers are often "absent from the table." Barbara Brittingham, Patricia O'Brien, and Julie Alig discuss the benefits to the institution of including institutional researchers in the accreditation process; they argue that such involvement will raise the visibility of institutional researchers and lead to IR's future involvement in other major campus initiatives. Jennifer Brown notes that there is a need for IR professionals to be fully engaged partners not only on their campus but also beyond their institution if they are to inform the discussions that have an impact on major new data collection efforts.

When institutional researchers are engaged partners, good things generally result. There are numerous examples of institutional researchers working with senior administrators to create management information

NEW DIRECTIONS FOR HIGHER EDUCATION, no. 141, Spring 2008 © Wiley Periodicals, Inc.
Published online in Wiley InterScience (www.interscience.wiley.com) • DOI: 10.1002/he.297

tools. A case in point is the dashboard that I created in conjunction with President Lawrence Bacow at Tufts University. For those unfamiliar with the concept of a dashboard, it is a succinct tool that can be used to inform viewers of the current state of affairs, yield information to evaluate performance, and help decision makers strategically guide the institution. The common denominator for all dashboards is a set of strategic indicators. Shortly after President Bacow arrived at Tufts, he requested that I develop a dashboard that he could regularly present to the board of trustees. We worked together to identify the critical variables that would be included, ones that reflected the strategic vision at Tufts and that would be of the most interest to trustees. The items that ultimately appeared on the dashboard fell into eleven categories: financial indicators, admissions statistics, enrollment, faculty, student outcomes, student engagement, student-faculty interactions, satisfaction measures, research activity, external ratings, and board activity. This was an enormously successful project, and it continues to be of great value to the president and the board.

I find institutional researchers to be collectively some of the hardest-working and most well-intentioned of professionals. In many ways, they are a profession that typifies the individual whom Marge Piercy describes in her poem "To Be of Use":

> I want to be with people who submerge
> in the task, who go into the fields to harvest
> and work in a row and pass the bags along,
> who are not parlor generals and field deserters
> but move in a common rhythm
> when the food must come in or the fire be put out.[1]

One of their overarching attributes is that most institutional researchers definitely want to be of use. They want to be of service to their institution and give faculty and administrators the information they need to make informed decisions. Sometimes it seems as if any question that is posed to an IR person is countered with another question. This is not because the institutional researcher is trying to be difficult; it is an attempt to gain clarity regarding what the requester really wants or needs. The world of higher education is complex, and even frequently used terms may mean different things to different people. Take as an example a seemingly simply request such as, "How many faculty do we have?" Without the institutional researcher gaining clarification, there could be many possible answers: "Are you interested in just the tenure-stream faculty? Are you interested only in those individuals who are engaged in instructional activities? What about adjunct faculty and those on sabbatical? Perhaps we should first discuss what question you are really trying to answer."

Examples regarding the complexity of the higher education enterprise abound. I could have given any number of examples of areas requiring clarity of definition before they are ready for decision making. Institutional researchers have long recognized this problem. In the late 1980s, discussion began among members of the IR community about creating a set of agreed definitions that would be used in supplying data to external agencies. What resulted from preliminary discussion was the Common Data Set (discussed by both Trainer and Brown in their chapters) and an ongoing dialogue with representatives from the Association of Institutional Research and the guide-book publishers.

Even in this time of extreme competition, institutional researchers are willing to share information with colleagues. This point is illustrated with a whimsical story recounted to me by my esteemed colleague Larry G. Jones, a senior public service associate emeritus from the Institute of Higher Education at the University of Georgia:

> I once had a colleague who by title and position ranked well over the Office of Institutional Research, who would call me into his office, lock the door, pull down the shades, close the curtains, and ask in a whisper if I could get some information from a sister institution without calling any attention to the request or the reasons for asking.
>
> When I told him I thought I could (and did so frequently when similar requests followed the same locked-door, pulled-shade, whispered requests for other information), I returned to my office, called my friend, and in thirty minutes or less (we usually had some gossip related to institutional research offices and friends to exchange) I had the information that was requested for her institution" [personal correspondence, January, 2008].

Trainer and Bers, in their respective chapters, discuss the institutional research culture of sharing. Not only do institutional researchers share comparative information about their respective institutions, they also share new ideas, practices, and techniques with one another. This enables IR to share with other members of their college and university campus cutting-edge best practices that can inform the community through lessons learned and promote models that can be applied to many programs.

Note

1. Alexa (http://www.americanpoems.com/poets/Marge-Piercy/17193).

INDEX

NEW DIRECTIONS FOR HIGHER EDUCATION
Order Form
SUBSCRIPTIONS AND SINGLE ISSUES

DISCOUNTED BACK ISSUES:

*Use this form to receive **20% off** all back issues of New Directions for Higher Education. All single issues priced at **$23.20** (normally $29.00). For a complete list of issues, please visit www.josseybass.com/go/ndhe.*

TITLE	ISSUE NO.	ISBN
_____	_____	_____
_____	_____	_____
_____	_____	_____

Call 888-378-2537 *or see mailing instructions below. When calling, mention the promotional code, JB7ND, to receive your discount.*

SUBSCRIPTIONS: *(1 year, 4 issues)*

☐ New Order   ☐ Renewal

U.S.	☐ Individual: $85	☐ Institutional: $209
Canada/Mexico	☐ Individual: $85	☐ Institutional: $249
All Others	☐ Individual: $109	☐ Institutional: $283

Call 888-378-2537 *or see mailing and pricing instructions below. Online subscriptions are available at www.interscience.wiley.com.*

Copy or detach page and send to:
John Wiley & Sons, Journals Dept, 5th Floor
989 Market Street, San Francisco, CA 94103-1741

Order Form can also be faxed to: 888-481-2665

Issue/Subscription Amount: $ _____	**SHIPPING CHARGES:**
Shipping Amount: $ _____	SURFACE Domestic Canadian
(for single issues only—subscription prices include shipping)	First Item $5.00 $6.00
Total Amount: $ _____	Each Add'l Item $3.00 $1.50

(No sales tax for U.S. subscriptions. Canadian residents, add GST for subscription orders. Individual rate subscriptions must be paid by personal check or credit card. Individual rate subscriptions may not be resold as library copies.)

☐ Payment enclosed (U.S. check or money order only. All payments must be in U.S. dollars.)

☐ VISA ☐ MC ☐ Amex # _____ Exp. Date _____

Card Holder Name _____ Card Issue # _____

Signature _____ Day Phone _____

☐ Bill Me (U.S. institutional orders only. Purchase order required.)

Purchase order # _____

Federal Tax ID13559302   GST 89102 8052

Name _____

Address _____

Phone _____ E-mail _____

JB7ND

NEW DIRECTIONS FOR HIGHER EDUCATION
IS NOW AVAILABLE ONLINE AT WILEY INTERSCIENCE

What is Wiley InterScience?

Wiley InterScience is the dynamic online content service from John Wiley & Sons delivering the full text of over 300 leading scientific, technical, medical, and professional journals, plus major reference works, the acclaimed *Current Protocols* laboratory manuals, and even the full text of select Wiley print books online.

What are some special features of Wiley InterScience?

Wiley InterScience Alerts is a service that delivers table of contents via e-mail for any journal available on Wiley InterScience as soon as a new issue is published online.
Early View is Wiley's exclusive service presenting individual articles online as soon as they are ready, even before the release of the compiled print issue. These articles are complete, peer-reviewed, and citable.
CrossRef is the innovative multi-publisher reference linking system enabling readers to move seamlessly from a reference in a journal article to the cited publication, typically located on a different server and published by a different publisher.

How can I access Wiley InterScience?

Visit http://www.interscience.wiley.com

Guest Users can browse Wiley InterScience for unrestricted access to journal Tables of Contents and Article Abstracts, or use the powerful search engine.
Registered Users are provided with a *Personal Home Page* to store and manage customized alerts, searches, and links to favorite journals and articles. Additionally, Registered Users can view free Online Sample Issues and preview selected material from major reference works.
Licensed Customers are entitled to access full-text journal articles in PDF, with select journals also offering full-text HTML.

How do I become an Authorized User?

Authorized Users are individuals authorized by a paying Customer to have access to the journals in Wiley InterScience. For example, a university that subscribes to Wiley journals is considered to be the Customer. Faculty, staff and students authorized by the university to have access to those journals in Wiley InterScience are Authorized Users. Users should contact their Library for information on which Wiley journals they have access to in Wiley InterScience.

ASK YOUR INSTITUTION ABOUT WILEY INTERSCIENCE TODAY!